KNUTE ROCKNE

A PICTORIAL HISTORY

Michael R. Steele

Sports Publishing, Inc.
Champaign, IL 61820

Interior designer and production coordinator: Deborah M. Bellaire and Erin J. Prescher
Editor: Susan M. McKinney
Dust jacket design: Julie L. Denzer

ISBN: 1-57167-255-9
Library of Congress Catalog Card Number: 98-89065

Photos courtesy of Notre Dame Sports Information Office, Notre Dame Photo Archives, College Hall of Fame Birger Rockne and Mike Pearson. We have made every effort to trace the ownership of all photos. If we have failed to give adequate credit, we will be pleased to make changes in future printings.

Printed in the United States.
www.SportsPublishingInc.com

This book is dedicated to my son

Sean Ryan Steele

I am so proud of you.
I love you always.

Set your sights high.
Give your best effort.
Never give up.
Find a way.
Always be positive.
Be faithful to Notre Dame.
Enjoy life to the fullest.
Always freely give and accept love.

TABLE OF CONTENTS

ACKNOWLEDGMENTS

In 1979, I heard from one of my former grad school professors, Russel B. Nye, who tipped me off about a pending series to be published about popular culture figures. Nye was one of the founders of the Popular Culture Association; he had previously won a Pulitzer Prize and was held in awe by several generations of students. He urged me to make a proposal to the publisher. Dutifully, I proposed a book on Knute Rockne, it was accepted, and published in 1983. Without Nye's generous, thoughtful recommendation, much in my life might not have ensued. I am forever in his debt.

A decade later, I was involved as a consultant on a documentary film about Rockne. Then Sagamore Publishing, under the leadership of the Bannon family, proposed reviving an older project, an *Encyclopedia* of Notre Dame football. That book has now gone into two editions, and I enjoy an excellent working relationship with Sagamore, with more books being planned even as this rewrite of the original Rockne book is being published. I am deeply indebted to Mike Pearson at Sagamore for his mentorship and sensible approach to this fascinating publishing field.

I am an academic, a professor of English and peace studies, with a special interest in Holocaust studies. Much of this work is sobering, with a high emotional price. My work in football is a healthy counterbalance to this … which my wonderful life partner, Gerianne, probably recognizes and fosters. I offer my sincere sense of my personal gratitude to her for her constant love, keen research skills, and kind support. Likewise, my four children see plenty of their father watching taped game replays and poring over game accounts from three-quarters of a century ago. I hope I've had enough time with them, but it has been hard.

I must also thank the many Notre Dame football players and members of the Notre Dame family who have been excellent and kind resources for me over the years: Moose Krause, Paul Castner, Chet Grant, Leon Hart, Brian Boulac, Rocky Bleier, Drew Mahalic, Jerome Heavens, and Bob Golic. Coach Dan Devine has recently been a fascinating, honest, thoughtful partner in a shared project. We have a friend, Lyn Leone, who has offered much assistance and timely support. Notre Dame's Sports Information Director, John Heisler, has always helped out, always kindly, often on short notice. Mike May in Sports Information has been very helpful and thoughtful. Jan Blazi, administrative assistant over the years to several Notre Dame head football coaches, has always found a way to put me in touch with the right people for various projects. Surely there are others, but these stand out.

Bernie Kish, Executive Director of the College Football Hall of Fame, has been very helpful at crucial stages of this project. His wise counsel and many connections to the world Rockne lived in opened up possibilities that would never have been attained otherwise.

Bernie led me to contact Knute Rockne's granddaughter, Anne Rockne-Volpe, who was most generous with her time and insights. Elaine and Frances Lubbers helped graciously with regards to the Rockne family home in South Bend and other matters.

Birger Rockne, a relative of Knute Rockne still living in Voss, and Svein Ulvund also of Voss, have been thoughtful and enthusiastic resources in this project, especially with regards to the acquisition of photographs from Voss. They have been good friends across the Internet and I wish them well and thank them sincerely.

I must recognize and applaud the excellent work of Murray Sperber, Professor of English and American Studies at Indiana University, who has worked fruitfully and insightfully in the Notre Dame archives, among other places. Prof. Sperber's work has shed accurate, new insights into the entire phenomenon of Notre Dame football. His work has corrected earlier mistakes in the public record, mine included. I am grateful to him for his outstanding contribution, especially for the clarity of vision and understanding to which his work leads readers.

My Dean at Pacific University, Tom Beck, puts up with my idiosyncracies in gentle fashion...and always manages to keep asking good sports trivia questions. I appreciate his friendship and good advice in ways he'll never know.

To one and all, please accept this expression of my sincere gratitude.

Voss, Norway, birthplace of Knute Rockne, present day.

INTRODUCTION

Fifty-three years before I entered Notre Dame as a freshman, Knute Rockne had made the same lonely trip from his home in Chicago to the campus just north of South Bend. Millions of students have made trips like this, from the familiar comfort of their homes to the strange experience of casting one's lot in with hundreds or even thousands of others in the same situation. While whole new intellectual, athletic, and social horizons are available, most first-year students find themselves wrestling with deeply personal issues, trying to find themselves, or ratifying the selves they brought to college.

Of this annual event, you can never absolutely predict who is going to succeed beyond anyone's wildest dreams. Some take the opportunity to try something new, or seek excellence where it had not been manifest before. Many never make the attempt to break out of their normal routines.

Knute Kenneth Rockne did not readily fit any predictable mold. He did choose a college that at the time took in some risky cases. In some ways, he was one of those risks, just as was George Gipp. Rockne seems to have had a sixth sense for landing in the right situation and then knowing what to make of it or how to maximize it. He eventually overcame early adversity and mistakes to make an indelible contribution to American culture.

That achievement was not gained without a certain price and without controversial results. Notre Dame may have reached the pinnacle it reached had Rockne not matriculated there. Collegiate football likely would have gone on in the direction that emerged as his teams knit together various intersectional rivalries. But Rockne added a certain flair and an attitude that served to captivate a large portion of the American mass entertainment market. He offered an articulate, passionate voice in defense of a particular approach to the education of the

whole person. He came to have a level of significance for millions of people that is rare in any field of endeavor.

It is remarkable to realize that a veteran postal clerk, a Scandinavian imigrant, went to college with his life

savings in 1910, initiating a sequence of events that would see him become one of the most famous Americans in

the first third of the twentieth century. With little more than a suitcase of modest possessions, lacking even a

diploma from high school, Knute Rockne thrust himself into and put his personal stamp on an entire game, in the

process turning it into one of this country's significant cultural features.

In a sense, this all began with a journey...and
ended with a journey. The journey that led Knute Rockne
to the forefront of American consciousness began with
the 1893 voyage from Norway to America. The airplane
flight that began in Kansas City in 1931 and ended in a
farmer's field less than an hour later, the crash that killed
Rockne, was the journey that ended his story. But beginnings are often endings, and endings are often new
beginnings. Rockne's appearance in this country as a
child was a beginning that signified the eventual end of a
certain kind of evolution to the game of football. His
death, a tragic ending to a life of unbelievable achievement, began a new phase of the social and cultural process where by Knute Rockne became an American icon.

What accounts for his enduring lagacy? It strikes
me that Rockne's memory benefits in obvious ways from
his continuing association with the University of Notre

Dame and its brilliant record of combining athletic and academic excellence. Rockne was also master of the art of manipulating the press. He knew how to cultivate his and his team's image to the remarkable benefit of both. But these are obvious matters. Almost anyone examining the record would arrive at these conclusions.

In my earlier examination of Rockne, upon which this book is based, it eventually struck me that Rockne was one of us—but launced to heights few could sustain. How many postal clerks have reached the pre-eminence this man achieved? Few do, but those singular examples take hold of the public's imagination as people invest themselves vicariously in these public lives. As I said in the 1983 version of the book, "He was kind of short, kind of bald, and kind of heart." That is, he looked like one of us, and endeared himself to us. He may have had some rough edges that have come to light, but his positive contributions far outweigh the problematic matters.

Thus, when we come to a full understanding and appreciation of Knute Rockne, we will have a better understanding of ourselves and of some of those important dynamics involved in our lives.

It started as a story that America has seen countless times … a family halfway across the world seeking to improve its lot. They made the decision to uproot themselves, leave their ancestral home, and make the long voyage across the ocean to the challenge and mystery of a new life. They did not live in poverty in their native country; indeed, they had all the trappings of middle-class respectability. They lived in a stable, peaceful northern European country, Norway. They were not escaping an oppressive regime nor religious persecution. Still, something burned within the heart and soul of Lars Rockne, perhaps inherited from his grandfather, Knute, who had felt restless enough in the early part of the nineteenth century while working the family farm to strike out on his own, independent of the family's long, loving relationship to the land, to rely solely on his substantial skills as a blacksmith and general mechanic. His shift away from farming Norway's rather thin soil to relying on his personal skills in servicing the needs of people portended Knute Rockne's choice three-quarters of a century later to leave behind chemistry and pharmacy studies to work closely with young athletes and provide a form of public entertainment for millions of Americans.

The Rockne family had been in Voss for several generations, enjoying its breathtaking site near towering mountains to the east—Hardangervidda—as well as the vista presented by the village, which was nestled along the shore of Vangsvatnet Lake. Centrally situated in the western districts of Norway, Voss lies about an hour's train ride east of Bergen, and about halfway between Norway's major fjords—Sognefjord to the north and Hardangerfjorden to the south.

Voss, Norway in 1895.

Lars Rokne's father, Knute Knutson Rokne, had taken the further initiative in 1852 to add a hardware store to the family's blacksmith shop. The family's work ethic developed a strong local reputation for superb machine work and repair, starting when Lars Rokne's grandfather had built and used a wheeled vehicle to replace the traditional Norwegian sled. Over the years, the Roknes developed a well-earned reputation for the quality of their craftsmanship in producing two-wheeled carriages. Kaiser Wilhelm of Germany took note and bought one of the carriages, and Lars won a prize for his workmanship at a Liverpool fair, both of which indicate that Lars was thinking big, far beyond the meadows, mountains and valleys, and beautiful fjords of Norway.

With his confidence increasing, Lars Rokne finally took the leap to go to America on his own where he displayed one of his handmade carriages at the 1893 World's Fair in Chicago. In so doing, Lars Rokne simply did what his Viking forebears had done—used masterful craftsmanship to create an aesthetically pleasing but highly functional means of transportation—then took it across the Atlantic. Fortunately for generations of American football fans, the family venture begun by Lars Rokne was a permanent move, unlike the Viking forays to North America.

The future Notre Dame football coach was born as the only son into this enterprising, gifted family on March 4, 1888. His father's 1893 trip to Chicago must have been nearly unbearable for the bright, inquisitive youngster. He seemed to like living on the edge a bit, and was wearing the new rubber boots his father had sent from America when he rode an ice floe out into the middle of a lake where boaters rescued him from further misadventure. His family must have worried about their only son during such escapades, and were perhaps a bit protective of him, but he really seems only to have been doing in a child's way what the Roknes had already been doing for many decades; pushing the envelope, showing a degree of restlessness and wanderlust. In many ways, this would prove to be a trait that the adult Knute Rockne (the family added the "c" after leaving Norway) would show on a daily basis … right to the day he died.

As a child, and perhaps into early adolescence, Knute Rockne was thought by his family to be a bit of a bumbler, a clumsy lad. In any case, he seems to have had a penchant for the colorful misadventure. With Rockne, it has always been difficult to sort fact from fancy. Various legends from his childhood add to the aura of the adult life: that he climbed to the crow's nest of the ocean liner as the vessel was still in the harbor at Bergen ... or that he fell into the frigid waters of the Bergen harbor ... or that it was perhaps the harbor in New York when young Knute clambered up the mast to the crow's nest. Then there was the time that Knute managed to get lost at the Chicago World's Fair after being in America only a short time and lacking in English skills, a little caper that must have driven his parents to sheer distraction.

But Knute Rockne was already showing the signs of being an adventurer with a flair for the dramatic, the grand gesture. He seemed to thrive on challenges, on new ventures. Moving from the rural town of Voss to one of America's exuberant, throbbing cities, Chicago, must have presented Knute with myriad opportunities for satisfying his need for exploration, investigation, and sheer curiosity. His forebears had to have been highly intelligent people; they had taken advantage of opportunities, mastered developing technologies, and flourished in the presence of risk. They had done this in a demanding environment that also required tremendous reserves of physical endurance and courage. They would have appreciated what Rockne was going to do with his life, al-

though it might have struck them as curiously unproductive in terms of the working world they inhabited.

But that difference, which allowed a bright, talented, hard-working immigrant to go to college, play a sport, and then make a career of and achieve national fame coaching that sport, was part of the emerging culture of late-nineteenth century America. Generations of immigrants to this country had had to serve their time grimly in the country's sweatshops, mines, and factories. They had faced grueling labor demands and worked themselves to early deaths so that their children might have advantages they had never enjoyed. Gradually, the relentless demands abated somewhat and it became possible to have greater access to an emerging

The young Rockne with two of his sisters.

array of entertainments, not the least being games—baseball, football, basketball, track and field. Americans thus set off in increasing numbers to become involved in the entertainment industry … sports to be sure, but also including what would become movies, theater, dance. Rockne would avail himself of all of these, even to the point of adding elements of drama and dance to the game of football. But more of that later.

The family's move from Voss, Norway, to Chicago took Rockne from a small village of a few dozen buildings near a rural lake to an emerging metropolis. All of Europe could be found in Chicago's ethnic neighborhoods. When Rockne's family moved to the Logan Square district, young Knute would find himself in a polyglot situation, with the usual animosities and dislikes between groups with differing national origins. With four sisters at home (Anna, Martha, Louise, and Florence) and no brothers, Knute seems to have invested himself heavily in a variety of youthful adventures with a distinctly adolescent male flavor to them.

A natural thing to do would be to engage his peers in sports. Baseball seems to have been Knute's original athletic love. The game, and its variations, can be played in virtually any location and in most conditions. Equipment can be nearly non-existent or elaborate. Rockne seems to have thrown himself into this game with great vigor, even as he also played neighborhood games of football. He could find games with other neighborhood baseball teams in the streets, in vacant lots, in parks, on school grounds.

But it was his parents who discouraged him from full involvement in football. No doubt they had grown aware of the concern many prominent Americans had regarding the sport … including President Theodore Roosevelt. Teddy Roosevelt, who had been a bit sickly as a youth but who had toughed his way past that problem, was a man not given to apologizing for the strenuous life. Still, even Teddy Roosevelt had to take notice when the style of play that dominated at the turn of the century ("mass play") more often than not resulted in disfigured faces, broken bones, paralysis, and even death. The game's equipment was minimal and primitive, macho attitudes prevailed, bulk was not unwelcome, and tactics were designed to bring tremendous weight and momentum to bear on a small point—often the poor lout with the ball. The game featured kicking, some

The youthful Rockne, perhaps before his nose met a baseball bat.

basic running plays, and brutal tackling. Finesse was unheard of.

Rockne was a small kid, perhaps 110 pounds when he entered high school, so football at first glance would not have seemed conducive to continued good health. His parents were truly looking out for their only son. Quite to the contrary of the brute physicality of turn-of-the-century football, his teachers had noted his sprightly intellectual gifts almost immediately. He had entered the American education system at Brentano grade school, where the teachers quickly perceived his great learning capacity, especially his impressive memory. Within two years, Knute was acknowledged as having the greatest capacity of their students. His best subjects were math and history—subjects that would serve well as important bases for future endeavors. Rockne would later show a strong aptitude for chemistry and had an avocational interest in military history and tactics. Both would play roles in his early career at Notre Dame.

The teenage Rockne and a tennis pal.

His intellectual and academic strengths would prove to be important components of the grown man. Father John Cavanaugh, the Notre Dame president who knew Rockne virtually all of his later life, once claimed that Rockne's elementary school grades were "close to the point of perfection." Cavanaugh found that Rockne's intellectual strengths were stunningly eclectic, the result of "a case of brain hunger" that would last until the end of his life. The child proved to be father to the man in that he loved to face and solve problems, find intriguing new ways of self-expression, blend seemingly disparate experiences into a unified whole, and, in general, apply brain power rather than brute force. This latter trait would prove to have tremendous impact in his playing and coaching the game of football.

But football had not yet become paramount for the young

Rockne. His solicitous parents remained adamant in their opposition to the game. To the untrained eye from the perspective of the sideline, football at the turn of the century must have seemed like complete mayhem. So, when Knute came home one day with his nose manifestly broken—by a baseball bat swung too close to his face in some fracas—the sheer irony of the situation apparently led his loving parents to relent in their objection to football.

So, with his ears taped up and with friendly policemen serving as amateur referees, the Norwegian Rockne threw his small, wiry, tough, and speedy frame into game action, playing as an end for the "Tricky Tigers," a neighborhood team apparently composed of "Swedes"—geography not being the strong suit in Logan Square at the time. Not much is known about the Tigers' tricks, but the adult Rockne would enjoy a well-earned reputation for tactical deceit in collegiate football, at least from the viewpoint of the many coaches who lost to his teams. His apprenticeship in football may have been on the informal side, but he seems to have learned highly significant lessons during this roughhouse period. One other irony from this period of Rockne's life must be mentioned: the Tricky Tigers, Swedes to the man, had as their main competition teams filled with Irish kids.

Being engaged in games like this helped acculturate youngsters informally into the mainstream of American life and culture. Rockne in later life liked to speak of his "baptism of mire" in Tricky Tigers games. Without a formal adult-directed coaching structure, youngsters were able to learn at first-hand important leadership skills, tactical decision-making, basic fairness and sportsmanship— all the while testing one's personal mettle. One can come to under-

Walter Eckersall would later be a favorite football referee for Rockne.

stand oneself in some essential ways. Significantly, during this period, Rockne began signing his first name as "Kanute" with a slash through the a to indicate that it was pronounced but not used in the spelling. Before too long, "Kanute" was anglicized into "Newt"—the name that has entered American history. His American personality was taking shape.

With his parents' objections overcome, Rockne's full initiation into the mystique of football as an important element of his life came when, as a young high school student, he had the chance to see a high school championship game between Brooklyn Prep from New York and the local Hyde Park High. The Chicago team was quarterbacked by the charismatic Walter Eckersall, who later gained fame as a player for Amos Alonzo Stagg at the University of Chicago. Eckersall personified all that Rockne later came to demand in a quarterback: a certain chestiness, tactical daring, and a genuine flair for command. Under Eckersall's relentless leadership, Hyde Park demolished Brooklyn Prep 105-0, a clear indication at the high school level that the balance of football power had definitely shifted, a process in which it moved westward, away from the original base it had held in the east. The later success of Notre Dame would make this trend a permanent feature of American collegiate football. Rockne was overwhelmed by Eckersall's heroic style of play. As he recounted in later years, he was particularly struck by the sense that Eckersall ran his team with all the timing of an orchestra's conductor, a revelation that provided a whole new level of meaning for him. This game also demonstrated to him that football could be an instrument for thinking, that the true appeal of the game was only latent in the mass play of the day. Rockne's early impressions from this game, with their emphasis on timing, rhythm, and thinking (as opposed to what Rockne later saw as bovine bulk and primitive brute force tactics) would lead ultimately to constant lessons impressed on his Notre Dame teams.

Unfortunately for Rockne's youthful aspirations, his diminutive size would not permit him to achieve football glory in high school. As a freshman, he was 5' 3" and 110 pounds. He managed only to play for the scrub team for Northwest Division High School. Harsh reality seems to have dominated in the remaining years of his high school career because Rockne apparently never made much of a mark in high school football. Instead, his natural gifts of sheer speed and leg strength led him to participate in track. He would eventually be timed at 4.6 seconds in the 40-yard dash and 2:02 in the half-mile, both commendable times at the turn of the century. He added pole-vaulting to his list of credits; his physical gifts of speed and good upper-body strength were a useful combination for this event.

Track and field, however, almost proved to be Rockne's undoing. It became such an obsession for him that his grades in school began to slip. Then he made a major error in judgment in the spring of 1905 by skipping classes in order to practice for an upcoming track meet. Along with several other miscreants, Rockne was caught and asked to transfer to another school. In a remarkable decision, he refused the transfer request and chose to leave high school without a diploma. It must have seemed to those closest to him that he had thrown away all he had worked for, that his potential would be tragically unfulfilled. His family had hoped he would attend college, perhaps in the footsteps of Eckersall at Chicago. The bright future that seemed imminent as a younger student must have appeared dim indeed.

In spite of this setback, the young man next showed what came to be known in later years as the Rockne drive. Following work at a variety of odd jobs, in 1907 Rockne sat for the Civil Service examination, hoping for employment with the U. S. Post Office. The examination included an essay section. Rockne chose to write about the need for a larger American navy in light of the recent Japanese victory over the Russian fleet. From this one can infer that Rockne kept abreast of the implications of international events, and that his keen interest in strategy, military history, and the relationship of war to contemporary life denoted a mind of considerable breadth for a young adult.

He was offered the Post Office job and began working on March 21, 1907, as a substitute clerk. On that same day, he was promoted to the position of a full clerk, for the less than princely annual salary of $600. It is not surprising that Rockne had not been wasting his time after the events of 1905. His Civil Service exam essay, with its focus on military policy and concerns, may be said to be a harbinger of events that would impact the lives of almost all Americans within the next decade, not to mention countless others in the Europe he had left behind as a child.

Rockne proved to be a success in his new job. Before long, he took on the additional responsibility as a dispatcher in the Mailing Division. He received annual raises until 1910, by which time he had saved enough money to attend college for a while. Nevertheless, he found himself badly underchallenged. He chafed under the working conditions fostered by an impersonal, inefficient bureaucracy. His personal enthusiasm in his approach to work, to his surprise, brought forth knowing smirks from older co-workers. The system was immune to the manifestation of personal merit; much of the work he eventually found to be uneven and unfair. Two things remained constant for him, even in this morass: he often managed to bring books to work so that he could keep his mind engaged, and he managed to stay in shape, in spite of the sedentary nature of the job, by running up and down in the building's driveway, dodging his slouching, startled co-workers with nifty moves.

From this point forward, it's difficult to separate his life from the culture he lived in. Clearly, Rockne had elements of Horatio Alger's heroes and their work ethic, and Frank Merriwell's earnestness and drive. These were among the operative social and cultural myths of America in 1910. Of course, there were harsh realities under the facade of progress, but Rockne was too busy being upwardly mobile to attend to them in any detail. His advice, in any case, would have been to work hard to overcome adversity. He was a charter member of the American Dream … good things would have to come his way eventually.

His job as a dispatcher in this "temple of loafing" demanded the daily use of the traplike memory his elementary teachers had earlier encountered. The job required him to memorize all the train schedules and their changes for all railroads in Illinois that traveled east. Later on, he claimed that doing this fostered the skills that were necessary in his job as a football coach. There he developed a justified reputation among his peers for mastering the tiniest detail.

While working for the Post Office, he kept in good shape by running in track meets for various clubs, such as the Irving Park Athletic Club, the Central YMCA, and, ultimately, the prestigious Illinois Athletic Club. At these competitions, he specialized in the half-mile and the pole vault. He filled out to his adult size of 5' 8" and 165 pounds … an average build to those who looked without paying much attention, but well-honed for athletic competition, and he was blessed with an impassioned desire to win. His aim was to keep himself well conditioned through track and, from his salary, save $1000 toward college expenses. He thought of going to the University of Illinois but, as he narrated later, felt that he would never realize fame in sports because college sports stars existed on pedestals in his imagination.

His participation in track during this period changed the course of his life forever. One of his sisters, he recalled, was adamant about the value of having a college education. In the early fall of 1910, Rockne claimed that he was at a track meet where he mentioned his college aspirations to two friends, Johnny Devine and Johnny Plant. Both attended Notre Dame, and they convinced Rockne that he would be better able to find the work he would need to afford college and, in general, would find it less expensive than Illinois (one can only marvel at the changes in this regard since Rockne heard this appeal).

Devine and Plant, however, were not off base in their assessment. Notre Dame had had an unstated policy that students from relatively poor backgrounds would be given every opportunity to meet college expenses through working various jobs around the campus. For the most part, the student body in 1910 came from the poor but upwardly mobile Catholic populations of the big cities. It had been founded in 1842 as a boarding school by a visionary, dedicated French priest, Father Edward F. Sorin, of the Congregation of the Holy Cross. It promised a rigorous but clean collegiate atmosphere and prided itself on being a "masculine democracy." It forbade social fraternities … the Greek organizations that would be so prominent at many colleges in the next few decades. Situated in north-central Indiana, ninety miles east of Chicago and three miles north of the quietly industrial town of South Bend (home to the Studebaker Corporation), it offered little (as generations of Notre Dame students have learned) in the way of "distractions."

Notre Dame's first intercollegiate football game was played against Michigan in an 8-0 loss on November 23, 1887, less than six months before Knute Rockne was born. In the twenty-one seasons in which the university fielded teams from 1887 to 1909, it had won 95 games, lost 30, and tied 10, for an impressive winning percentage of .760 (a figure which Notre Dame football teams have maintained since then, the highest such percentage among major colleges in the history of the game). It had played some major schools and other schools on the rise. For instance, it had defeated Michigan Agricultural College (now Michigan State) in 1898, 1899, and 1902 by an aggregate score of 126-0. Some of its opponents were mere cannon fodder, such as hapless American Medical which, in the seasons of 1903-05, lost three games to Notre Dame by the humiliating total score of 286-0.

The famous Red Salmon, a Walter Camp third team All-America choice in 1903 as a fullback (Camp was notoriously prejudiced toward eastern schools in these selections) captained the team in 1902 and 1903, leading the team in the latter season to an undefeated, unscored-upon slate. In 1909, the Irish had upset an overconfident Michigan team (and genuinely upset Michigan coach Fielding Yost in the process, who kept the two teams away from each other for more than thirty years after the 1909 Wolverine debacle). This 1909 Notre Dame team, boasting a 7-0-1 record, claimed the Western championship by virtue of this win over Michigan and its point total of 236 to 14.

In spite of these stellar achievements, and the university's proximity to Chicago, Rockne claimed to know almost nothing about Notre Dame. That may have been the case for Rockne in 1910 (or, more likely, he knew how to embellish the story for his own purposes), but his decision to matriculate there would forever disabuse him of his supposed ignorance and alter irrevocably the course of intercollegiate football. However, apparently he was not fully convinced in September that college was going to be the place for him—he did not bother to make his

The center of the Notre Dame campus as Rockne would have seen it in 1910.

resignation official from the Post Office until well into November, an uncharacteristic demonstration of uncertainty on his part.

The arboreal beauty of the Notre Dame campus was Rockne's first impression. The magnificent golden-domed administration and classroom building, along with the beautiful French Gothic church, dominated the center of the campus in 1910 even more than they do today. Rockne had to take an entrance examination to make up for the lack of a high school diploma, but he had stayed mentally acute while working at the Post Office and he passed the test with ease. At the time the university had seven dormitories; Rockne was assigned to a single room in Brownson Hall—not the double room with Gus Dorais for his roommate as the myth would have it. Brownson Hall was located just behind the Administration building—the famous Golden dome, perpendicular to and arranged about in the middle of the larger building. Accordingly, Rockne would have had countless opportunities to be walking in the vicinity of the Dome and to be deeply impressed by its quiet majesty. Needless to say, this would also be an excellent opportunity for some of the mystique of the place to rub off on him.

Ben Franklin once observed that a baby doesn't have much to recommend it. Likewise, Rockne's arrival at Notre Dame, the start of a relationship between man and place that would last more than twenty years, was inauspicious yet a bit odd. He had arrived with his life savings of $1,000, one modest suitcase, and the woolen suit he was wearing. He knew only Plant and Devine. He was prematurely balding and must have been aware of seeming rather old to the other freshmen. He was an Evangelical Lutheran in a place rooted deeply in French and Irish Catholicism. The Post Office years had worked lines into his face by the age of twenty-two. Above all, he worried.

No one could have known it, least of all Rockne himself, but in spite of his concerns, he was starting something that would mark forever American institutions—this university, the game of football, its acceptance by tens of millions of fans, even the presidency of the country itself. He could not have known it, and the university would mourn of it, but Rockne had already lived more than half of his life when he first stepped foot on Notre Dame soil. In an intriguing way, Rockne's life journey had started on Norwegian soil, near the land his family had farmed for generations, and now had taken him to the flatlands of northern Indiana, where a university rose out of the earth. Rockne would come, eventually, to so love this Indiana earth that he would kneel down and kiss it under the goalposts of the field where his teams played. And he would die crashing to the earth of a Kansas farm, a victim of man's technological hubris in the face of far stronger natural forces.

But much of that yet lay ahead of him. In 1910, Notre Dame enrolled 400 students. Almost all of them met the university's rigorous physical education requirement by playing either varsity football or "inter-hall ball." Brownson Hall had fielded the first intramural team in the late 1880s, when a Brother Paul organized the first campus team. Dutifully, Rockne tried out for the 1910 Brownson Hall team. This was good football, with teams composed of athletes that many colleges would have been glad to have, but these players had chosen to give it a try at Notre Dame, perhaps just to stay in touch with the competition they loved during their college studies, or as a launching pad to the various levels of the varsity team. There is also the view that the elaborate intramural system

Looking up at the Dome—as Rockne would have see it on his way to Brownson Hall.

of athletics at Notre Dame is a necessary diversion for the undergraduates, to burn off their extra energy supply, making them more manageable for the priests and professors.

In addition to the all but mandatory participation in some form of football at the university, Rockne also worked in the chemistry labs as a janitor. He almost left the university during his first month there when some sacramental wine was stolen from a lab for which he was responsible. Notre Dame has always had very strict regulations providing for summary expulsion in the case of proven theft, so Rockne was right to be concerned about his status. He packed his only suitcase. But Gus Dorais, Plant, and Fred Steers intercepted him and talked him into staying.

So, in little more than a month, Rockne seems to have made contact with football people who would

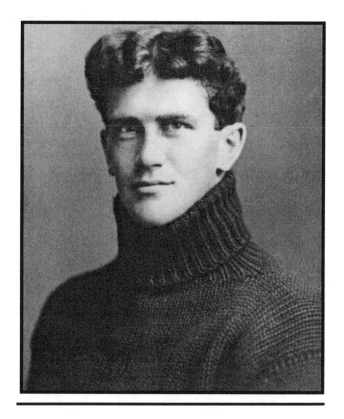

Shorty Longman, Rockne's first football coach in college.

loom large for him in the next few years. By October, he seems to have already tried out for the varsity football team. The Brownson Hall team was coached by a varsity player, Joe Collins, who played left end for the Irish. Collins noted Rockne's ability (in spite of the fact that Rockne had not played organized football for the better part of a decade, which says something about his drive, competitiveness, and conditioning) and recommended to Head Coach Shorty Longman that Rockne have a tryout. Longman had played fullback for none other than Fielding Yost at Michigan, from 1903 to 1905, and he seemed to like smash-mouth football … in a 1909 blowout win over a much smaller opponent, he had let his big linemen romp for five touchdowns. When Notre Dame hired him away from Wooster College (where Longman coached Wooster to an upset win over Ohio State), it was making the conscious choice to replace an easterner, Dartmouth's All-American Victor Place, with a coach with roots firmly planted in the midwest, yet another sign of the game's evolution away from eastern influences.

So, Rockne gave it a try. From his account, told and retold countless times in later years as his fame grew exponentially, he was an abysmal failure in his early efforts for the Longman and the Irish. He had been an end for the Tricky Tigers back in Logan Square, in what must have seemed like a totally different life to Rockne. Here, in organized collegiate football, Longman had him try out for his old Michigan position—fullback. You did not have to be a Larry Csonka or Jim Brown then to be a fullback. One of Notre Dame's all-time great players, Red Salmon, roughly a contemporary of Longman's, was only 5' 10" and 165 pounds when he gave intercollegiate football a try a decade earlier. Playing fullback did, however, require an absolutely fierce willingness "to buck the line," throwing oneself with abandon among the behemoths of the trenches. Since baseball had already rearranged his face, perhaps Rockne did not have to worry too much about what little protection old leather helmets afforded the face.

Rockne played well at fullback, in spite of his later accounts. In one instance, he ran for three touchdowns against the freshman team. He worked well enough to make the team as the third-string fullback, no small achievement given his comparative lack of experience. It's not hard to imagine what he brought to the task—a strong frame, a big heart, superb conditioning, tremendous dedication and self-discipline, a fierce love of competition.

FOOTBALL SQUAD 1910

The 1910 Notre Dame team; Rockne first on left, seated second row.

It is interesting to consider why he would downplay his achievement later in life. Obviously, it is was not his way to brag. He seldom did that anyway. He liked to make himself the butt of various jokes and anecdotes. Rockne characteristically set himself up as an easy mark, only to prove quite the opposite. It may have been his way of taking advantage of a competitor's willingness to misconstrue signals and data. Rockne showed a tendency all of his life to engage his mind in partnership with his body, creating a difficult combination to beat. Those who entered a contest against him without the proper mental equipment were going to have a long day. Furthermore, Rockne enjoyed and involved himself in various dramatic productions, as we shall see, and helped beat Army in 1913 by faking a leg injury. Finally, Rockne's habitual self-effacement may be seen as another component in his Horatio Alger-like approach to life, relentlessly overcoming weakness and obstacles to come out on top. If it seems that he had started from an inferior position, the final achievement stands out all the more.

Strangely, the Rockne we have come to know—a raconteur, a showman, a man skillful with the media, one of the most famous faces in American sports—may have had a shy side to his personality. He may have constructed an elaborate structure of truths, half-truths, and fictions to keep prying eyes from coming too close to the essential man. The public man may have belonged to the masses, but there was a complex maze to weave through to get any closer than what one saw or heard publicly. Perhaps the real Knute Rockne was the quiet man who gently tended to his backyard vegetable garden—although even there he won first prizes. But it wouldn't do to have the masses trampling around in that vegetable garden.

In any case, Rockne's collegiate football career was started. In the course of his undergraduate days at Notre Dame, the Irish would win 24 games, lose 1, tie 3. Rockne would start at left end for three varsity campaigns, from 1911 to 1913. Those teams never lost a game. The aggregate

Rockne in his senior year at Notre Dame.

score for that period is an astonishing 879 points for Notre Dame to 77 for the opposition. The average score was 40-3. Typical results included an 80-0 rout of Loyola of Chicago in 1911; a 116-7 extermination of St. Viator and a 69-0 slaughter of Marquette, both in 1912; and an 87-0 demolition of Ohio Northern in 1913. But the Irish also met and defeated tougher opposition: 3-0 over Pittsburgh in 1912, and 14-7 over Penn State and 30-7 over Texas in 1913.

For his three varsity seasons from 1911 to 1913, Rockne would play for two other head coaches: Jack Marks, from Dartmouth, replaced Longman for the 1911 and 1912 campaigns, and Jesse Harper, from Indiana's Wabash College, took the reins in 1913. The order of the day for the 1911 Irish was team speed. The team's only 200-pounder was fullback Ray Eichenlaub; otherwise, Marks had a bunch of small overachievers. Rockne fit right

Captain Rockne, enjoying fame as a college senior.

in. The Irish under Marks unveiled an early version of a shift tactic—the backfield moving quickly to a new position just prior to the snap of the ball—which would be a feature of Notre Dame football for more than thirty years, brilliantly exploited and improved by Rockne in his thirteen years as Notre Dame's head coach. In 1911, his sophomore year, the Irish went undefeated, with only one touchdown scored against them all season, in a 32-6 win over Ohio Northern, on an official's mistake in not calling a batted-down pass incomplete. An ONU player scooped up the ball and took it into the end zone. Rockne lost a chance to enter the scoring record book (and win the game) in a 0-0 tie with Pittsburgh when he lost a 40-yard TD runback of a loose ball when the official (always the officials!) ruled that the whistle to start the play had never blown. The Irish had another scare that year in a 6-3 win over in-state rival Wabash College. Wabash would have won the game under rules adopted later when they lost a TD on a pass that went more than 20 yards—illegal in 1911. Notre Dame officials remembered the game and the wily opposing coach—Jesse Harper—would be hired to lead the Irish in Rockne's senior year.

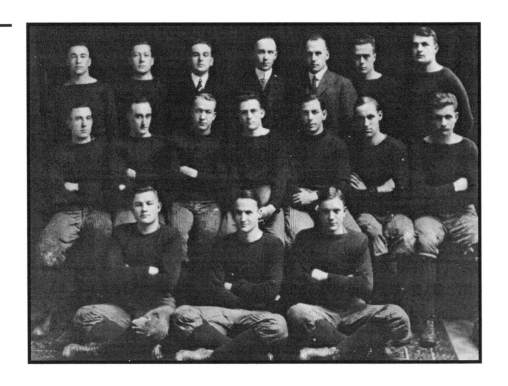

The 1912 Notre Dame football team.

The 1912 season saw football's scoring values fixed at the values known today, except for the 2-point conversion, added in 1958. Marks stayed with his small, fast team concept, with Eichenlaub for a lasting impression if needed. The Irish decimated St. Viator in the opener 116-7; the Saints turned out to be both smaller and slower, an unfortunate combination. Of the nineteen TDs the Irish scored in the game, fifteen were tallied by four players, with Heine Berger garnering five and Eichenlaub three more. That Rockne at end seems not to have been invited to the TD party still shows that the passing game had not fully evolved in spite of the fact that the forward pass had been legalized in 1906. The 1912 Irish administered a stern 41-6 rebuke to Harper and his

Jesse Harper, Rockne's coach for his senior
football campaign.

Wabash hopefuls, although it was a close game into the third quarter.
Rockne made a strong contribution in a 3-0 Irish win over Pittsburgh
with a 33-yard pass reception and his usual sterling defensive play. The
Irish ended the 1912 season undefeated and untied, going 7-0, the
first time for Notre Dame since a one-win season in 1889.

Jack Marks moved on and Notre Dame officials jumped at the
opportunity to invite Wabash's Jesse Harper to coach the football team
and serve as Athletic Director. He had impressive credentials: he had
played quarterback for Stagg at Chicago from 1902 to 1905, subbing
for Rockne's boyhood hero, Walter Eckersall; he played baseball for
Stagg; he first coached football at Alma College in Michigan, losing
only three games in four years; his 1907 baseball team won the Michigan state championship, beating the Wolverines in the process; at
Wabash, he defeated Purdue three out of four tries.

Harper inherited a mature, talented Notre Dame team, led by
Captain Rockne. He took the shift a step closer to the perfection that
Rockne would reach, and he added a sophisticated passing game. Rockne's first game in his senior year was an 87-0 pasting of Ohio Northern; there was no need to showcase the aerial offense. South Dakota was another matter—they took an early lead, but Eichenlaub hammered in a score, Dorais hit two field goals, then added a 40-yard TD pass to take the covers off a fine-tuned, well-integrated running and passing game that kept the South Dakota

The undefeated 1913 Fighting Irish,
Knute Rockne, Captain.

Knute Rockne, master of all he surveys.

defense at bay most of the game. It would have been a good game for Army to scout, but they didn't—and paid the price later for the omission. Besides, Rockne was injured and missed the game, so an Army scout would have never seen what he could do. He made it back for the next game, a 62-0 rout of Harper's former team, Alma, and played a great all-around game—solid defense, crisp blocking, zippy end runs, pass receptions snagged during precise pass routes. Army did scout this game, but Notre Dame was able to keep it pretty simple since Alma never mounted a serious threat.

Rockne's grandest moment as a player came in Notre Dame's shocking 35-13 victory over Army on November 1, 1913, the victory that forever changed the game of football. As far as football history is concerned, this game cannot be overestimated for its impact and influence on subsequent developments. It has, quite simply, become part of the cultural mythology of America. The story does not even require the rhetorical flourishes of a Rockne to be appreciated. The U. S. Military Academy in particular and the East in general were distinctly underwhelmed by the opportunity to play little-known Notre Dame, a team coming from, as the accounts had it, South Bend, Illinois. So much for geography and accuracy in reporting. Only second-rate reporters were sent to cover the game.

It was a fluke of scheduling in the first place. Army had been dropped from the schedules of two other schools, including Yale, due to its less than rigorous eligibility rules (players who had played elsewhere, and even graduated, could still play for Army until their military training was completed … somewhat akin to the football nomads who roamed the country in prior decades playing for seven or eight varsity seasons). So, Army badly needed opponents to fill out its schedule. Jesse Harper heard of the opportunity late in 1912 and

Gus Dorais, four-year starter at quarterback for Notre Dame, 1910-1913.

Game action from the Irish win over Army in 1913 ... Rockne scoring with a pass.

jumped at it. Officials at Notre Dame felt vindicated in hiring Harper partially for his business acumen when Army agreed to pay Notre Dame $1000 for coming to the plains above the Hudson.

Cadet Omar Bradley saw the visitors working out the day before the game. Had he looked closely, he would have seen that four Irish players were not wearing the usual cleats ... Notre Dame only had 14 pairs for its 18 players. Instead, he was a bit mystified by what he thought was some sort of juggling act. The Irish weren't juggling, however, just practicing their pass routes and receiving Dorais's throws.

Ironically, Army was the best passing team in the East. But the essence of their game was akin to the old mass play that Rockne had seen as a youngster. Forward passes were not an integral part of their game plan, but were deployed only when the Cadets were in dire straits. Basically, the pass had no tactical value in the sense of being part of a planned attack against an opposing defense. They just heaved the ball to gain ground quickly when all else had failed.

In the game, Army seemed to take command early on by virtue of its superior size, using its ground game almost exclusively. Rockne had spent this early part of the game lulling the Cadet secondary defenders with a fake limp. The first Irish score followed an 85-yard drive, keyed by passes from Dorais to halfback Joe Pliska and Rockne, capped by Pliska's 5-yard TD run. Army scored twice with its running game in the second quarter, but Rockne staked the Irish to a 14-13 halftime lead with a 25-yard TD reception, leg now healed. As the half ended, Harper had quarterback Dorais and his center on one side of the field, near the sideline, and the other nine men wide on the opposite side, for a long pass, but Army intercepted. In the third quarter, Army reached the Irish 2-yard line, but Rockne stopped a Cadet runner, then made a sack on the next play, setting up a rare Army pass that Dorais intercepted for a touchback. Eichenlaub scored on the resulting possession. The befuddled Cadets surrendered another TD on a pass to Pliska, and Eichenlaub closed out the Irish scoring, and Army's hopes, with

Halfback Joe Pliska later in life.

the last Irish TD on a run for the 35-13 final score. Dorais burned the Cadets for 243 yards with 14 completions in 17 attempts, including the longest pass play in Irish annals to date, a 40-yarder, to Rockne.

The Cadets had given it a good shot; they did try to make adjustments to the Irish attack. But when they widened out to defend passes, Eichenlaub would hammer a run or Pliska would slash outside. If they played tight to stop the run, Dorais would strike their vulnerable defense with a pinpoint pass. Modern football was born with this kind of tactical maneuvering.

The Irish next played and defeated Penn State, the first home loss for the Nittany Lions since 1894. Winning 14-7, the Irish were helped by a short TD pass to Rockne to go with an Eichenlaub TD run. After

Game action of the 1913 Irish against Texas. Rockne in lower left looking up.

beating a scrappy Christian Brothers team in St. Louis, Notre Dame toppled Texas 30-7, using 77 runs and 10 pass completions in 21 attempts. Eichenlaub and Dorais made All-American teams and Rockne garnered third-team All-America notice from Walter Camp himself, probably reluctant recognition that Eastern football's long-time prominence and domination now faced a serious challenge.

Harper's 1913 Irish had taken advantage of football rules changed in 1906, partially due to the influence of Teddy Roosevelt's political pressure designed to reduce the kinds and numbers of major injuries created by mass play tactics. Thus legalized, even with certain restrictions, the forward pass was taken up as a serious offensive weapon by Eddie Cochems, the head coach at St. Louis University. His team had gone undefeated in 1906, outscoring the opposition by 402-11.

Obviously, Rockne did not invent the forward pass. He always gave proper credit to Cochems, Glenn Warner, and Stagg for this aspect of the evolution of the game. But Warner and Stagg were primarily involved in the rules changes; Cochems put them to good use as a head coach. Rockne's contribution was in the physical execution of the play as a receiver. When the 1913 Irish squad traveled east to meet Army, they were going into a section of the country that had not, for various reasons, eagerly accepted the forward pass as a tactical device. Perhaps the East was trapped in its own history, unable to see the potential for football's progress in the new rules changes. The football itself in use at that time was not well designed for the passing game; it was one and a half inches larger in circumference than the modern ball adopted for use in the mid-1930s. Finally, and most crucially, it was not thrown or caught in a manner very familiar to viewers of the modern game. Rockne once observed that the reigning method of the day was that the football was more or less thrown like a medicine ball. The putative receiver would maneuver to a designated place, turn, stop, and wait for the ball.

The immortal Amos Alonzo Stagg.

Rockne's contribution was to enhance this primitive notion of a pass pattern, to catch the ball with loose hands and relaxed fingers, and to do so on the dead run after having executed a precise pattern as part of the play's larger picture, a pattern designed to keep the defender guessing. In a 1951 letter to football historian Allison Danzig, Rockne's quarterback, Gus Dorais, averred that Rockne developed the modern conception of the passing lanes and route tree that depended not on mere speed but on running cuts, angles, and changes of pace. (We can only wonder if all this was somehow first implemented by Rockne in his days dodging co-workers at full speed when he was running to stay in shape at the Post Office). During Rockne's tenure as head coach, he would develop this passing strategy for Notre Dame backs and ends to a point of sophistication not reached elsewhere until more than two decades after his death.

It is important to recognize that there was much more to Knute Rockne while attending college than mere football exploits. The list of other accomplishments is extensive and reveals a multi-talented person: he played the flute for the campus orchestra; participated in track and field (including coming close to current records for the pole vault); edited Notre Dame's student yearbook as a senior; boxed in smokers in the South Bend area, with Dorais as his manager, and played semi-pro football, both to pick up extra money; acted in several campus theatrical productions; founded the Monogram Club Absurdities; and compiled an academic record with a double major in pharmacology and chemistry, garnering magna cum laude honors at graduation (with a 90.52 average, out of 100, for his four years). He worked with, studied under, and knew well Father Julius Nieuwland, whose

The graduate.

Knute and Bonnie Rockne.

research led to the invention of synthetic rubber, who thought Rockne to be one of the most impressive students in his many years of teaching. It had not been an altogether easy thing to do, especially in the low moments following his father's death in 1912, but Rockne graduated from Notre Dame on June 15, 1914.

From Notre Dame, Rockne moved on to St. Louis. There he took on a high school coaching job and applied to medical school at St. Louis University. The admissions committee's decision was negative; the combination of coaching and a rigorous medical school curriculum did not seem promising or possible. This may reveal a certain level of naiveté on Rockne's part. The world had been his oyster for a few years. Perhaps all things seemed possible to him, but Horatio Alger mythology has its limits. Rockne was back in South Bend in short order.

There he had some more decisions to make. Harper knew of some jobs. Rockne's close friend, Gus Dorais, took a coaching job at St. Jospeh's College in Iowa, supposedly winning the choice with a coin flip. But Harper wanted Rockne as an assistant coach anyway. A deal was worked out in which Rockne would serve as head track coach, assistant football coach, and chemistry instructor for Notre Dame's prep students. All this came about very quickly. . . only one month after graduating from Notre Dame, Rockne went to Cedar Point, Ohio, (where he had been a lifeguard in the summer of 1913) and married Bonnie Gwendolen Skiles there on July 15, 1914.

Knute Rockne was now fully ensconced in the Notre Dame orbit. He had shown up on campus four years earlier carrying most of his life's valuables with him. He had scraped and scrapped, making ends meet in licit and, occasionally, less than licit

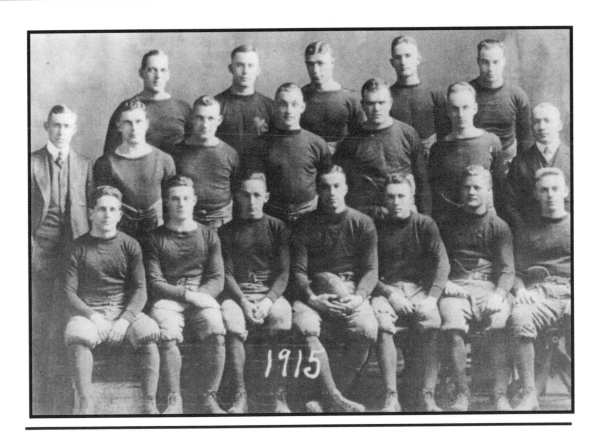

The 1915 Fighting Irish football team.

ways. He made an impression on the place at the time, to be sure, but it had reciprocated and had its lasting effect on him. Always a restless soul, Rockne would flirt with other schools in future years, but he never could make the final break. So, during the summer after his graduation, he wed the love of his life and took the first career step that would make him a permanent fixture in the history of the university. He had enjoyed a measure of fame as an undergraduate, certainly more than most collegians ever have, and he could have put it behind him and moved on to other realms. For most people, life must ultimately be lived away from one's school days. But Rockne's life would never be separated from the collegiate world ... although his devotion to and defense of athletics would eventually take on proportions that became controversial in the world of academe. To this day, there are tensions, at Notre Dame but also at virtually all major institutions that have football, over the matter of resource allocation and the role of such major sports. Rockne, as we shall see, contributed directly to this tension through his vigorous defense of football in the face of its critics and his national prominence, for the bright fame he experienced briefly in 1913 was a mere glimmer compared to what lay ahead.

Rockne's four years as Harper's assistant (1914-1917) allowed him to consolidate coaching techniques and his ideas about tactics. He was able to serve an apprenticeship under a very worthy mentor in Harper. The Notre Dame administration had hoped that Harper would find a way to impress Notre Dame's credentials upon the representatives of the Western Conference (today's Big 10) for eventual admittance ... but this hope failed. Harper did succeed, however, in expanding the football schedule to include more of the major schools: Yale,

Stan Cofall, dependable halfback for Notre Dame, 1914-16.

Syracuse, Nebraska, and Rice, in addition to what soon amounted to an annual tilt with Army, as well as teams that were major powers during the period but have slipped into football oblivion since—Haskell, Carlisle, and Washington and Jefferson. Harper's five years directing the football fortunes of Notre Dame produced results and statistics that compare favorably with others in the Irish pantheon. Harper's won-loss record stood at 34-5-1 (.871 for a winning percentage, just behind Frank Leahy's .888 and Rockne's amazing .897 among coaches with a tenure of five years or more at Notre Dame … one might consider Lou Holtz's .765 after 11 seasons under the Dome, modestly ahead of the school's .759 winning percentage for 1,010 games through the 1997 Independence Bowl game). Harper's teams scored 1,219 points to the opposition's 170; the average score was 30-4. One of Harper's teams was undefeated; two teams lost only one game; the 1916 squad had eight shutouts in nine games. Of the 26 head coaches in Irish history, Harper ranks fourth in average winning margin—defeating teams by more than 26 points per game on average, a full 10 points more than Rockne's teams would manage, 9 points more than Leahy and Parseghian would compile. In his five seasons, six of his players earned various All-American awards. So, Rockne had as his mentor one of the most effective coaches in Notre Dame's history.

Harper entrusted Rockne with some of his duties if the situation warranted it. In one 1916 game, Rockne was given the coaching duties because Harper was bedridden with a serious cold. The opponent was Wabash, Harper's previous school, not exactly a threat to the Irish. This game provides an early example of Rockne's oratory. Cy DeGree, the right guard for the Irish, told Francis Wallace, who observed the Notre Dame scene for many years, that Rockne's pre-game pep talk described in horrific detail the diabolical devices that the Little Giants might use against the Irish, that every Notre Damer would be needed to give a total effort in order to squeak past Wabash, which probably had recruited berserkers to play. Rockne had himself worked up into a fever pitch and concluded his oration with the cry, "Now go out there and crucify 'em!!" With that demand ringing in their heads, the Irish methodically dispatched Wabash by a 60-0 score.

If this is any indication, Rockne still clearly had a few things to learn yet with regard to the finer points of motivational technique. DeGree concluded that this case revealed Rockne's inspirational potential and charismatic personality. The matter, if not the art, he seems to have learned from Shorty Longman, who habitually reminded his players, week after histrionic week, that their current opponent constituted the ultimate crisis of their young athletic lives. One can imagine what this rhetoric must have initially meant to impressionable freshmen. But Longman either did not or could not vary the script, and his players were soon nodding in spite of the din. Later, Rockne suggested that one such stemwinder per season was about all a team could absorb and still have it be effective as a motivational device.

Harper, who was more the straight man to Rockne's motivational pyrotechnics, let Rockne give the pregame talk once again that season, before the Nebraska game. It worked well enough for a 20-0 win, but Murray Sperber has noted that Rockne seems to have had some money riding on this game—and kept the starters in long enough to insure beating the point spread. This was a good bit before the creation of the NCAA as we know it, but the kinds of stories that veterans from this era can tell are enough to make most sports fans shudder. Rockne definitely had his public persona, but he also operated comfortably in the smoke-filled rooms, as it were, where he had made a modest living as a club boxer. He frequented the South Bend pool hall known as Hullie and Mike's, and surely became acquainted there and elsewhere with a wide variety of specimens from the different strata of the social spectrum.

In any case, the 1916 Nebraska win perhaps taught Rockne the lesson that it was best not to overindulge in the matter of giving bombastic motivational exhortations in routine fashion. In his thirteen seasons (1918-

Rockne in a practice session.

1930) as head coach of the Irish, it has been estimated that he gave about eight or nine crucifixion-type demands. Most of these are more or less on the record. It was more normal for him to do the usual routine—reminding players of their assignments, reviewing the opposition's key personnel, all mixed in with a bit of Norwegian blarney. It is doubtful if he could ever stop being the showman, the ring master, completely.

Rockne's impact on Notre Dame football as an assistant coach went a good deal beyond his tentative efforts at locker-room oratory. He was instrumental in devising a variation on Stagg's shift in suggesting that the backfield emphasize perfection of timing in the shift to get the jump on the defense before it could react effectively to the shifting backs. Unlike today's football, the center on a team that used such a shift had to be able to hike the ball at different angles in order to hit different backs at various distances on the several plays used in a game.

A no-nonsense Rockne.

This allowed the ballcarrier to reach the point of attack with more blockers more quickly than with any other type of offense in use at the time.

Having toiled for the Irish as an end, Rockne had insights into that position that contributed to a devastating innovation in the basic tactic of the shift. This was his idea to shift ("flex") the ends wider or tighter in relation to the tackles, in synchronization with the backfield, creating a variety of improved blocking angles. Rockne, as an end, had played a line position and would often have to mix it up with much larger men, so he found it necessary to refine his own blocking techniques, especially when overmatched physically. He had evolved a technique known then as "boxing tackle." His boxing experience easily translated into the use of head feints as well as the use of the opponent's bulk and forward charge for leverage in order to deliver a block or avoid a block and be in position for the tackle. The flexing ends and the shifting backfield provided as many as five or six blockers concentrated at a point against an overwhelmed defense for maximum blocking effectiveness.

His blocking philosophy, it is important to realize, did not rely on double-teaming defensive players. Instead, he taught brush-blocking or influence blocking, in which the blocker brushed or nudged the defensive player out of the optimum position for stopping the offensive play. Or the blocker "read" the defensive player's charge and allowed him to move in the general direction that he wants to go if it is not likely to stop the play's unfolding. The result was that the defensive player either overran the play or was taken away from it, as the play's flow went away from him. In this way, the defensive player basically nullified himself, and the blocker was not required to make repeated excessive demands on himself to achieve his objective.

Another advantage to the blocking system taught by Rockne was that, once the ball carrier reached the point of attack at the line of scrimmage, if the blockers had done their jobs, then there were a couple of blockers remaining for downfield blocking. This was the beginning of what came to be known as "the perfect play." If the shift had succeeded in catching the defense napping, if the blockers executed their jobs as assigned, and if the runner read the running lane correctly, there was nothing left to do but score a touchdown. This became a characteristic feature of Notre Dame teams coached by Rockne and an integral part of his football philosophy. In essence, this meant that a touchdown could be scored by Notre Dame from almost any point on the football field

(an approach to the game that seems to have filtered from Rockne to Jimmy Crowley to Vince Lombardi). The pressure this put on a defense was enormous; any lapse in execution could have disastrous consequences due to the advantage provided by the shift at the point of attack. The long gainer happened frequently for Rockne's teams. He believed that it was actually far more difficult to score from a short distance away from the end zone—the offense's options are minimized and deception is less likely to occur.

This approach to the game became known as the "Rockne system" and was contrasted to the "Warner system," which depended less on deception and more on long, steady marches with the advancement of the ball depending on a series of short gains, which also consumed clock time with its methodical drives. The latter also featured a wingback system, with the fullback playing a crucial role in the passing game in addition to the running game. Rockne's system, as mentioned, employed the shift and featured the left halfback, although any man in the backfield could (and did) throw passes. The two systems, and their inventors, clashed in the 1925 Rose Bowl when the Irish met and

Knute Rockne and Pop Warner.

defeated Warner's Stanford team. Stanford's game statistics clearly show that they did phlegmatically cover ground. But football is not entirely a territorial game, nor a clock game. Rockne's teams could strike for a score at any time, and often did. Teams that did not feature this had to rely on field position, although an opponent with a good punter and defense could turn this strategy against them. Rockne's approach was appreciated more by the fans because it provided dramatic, seemingly unpredictable turns of events that could dishearten an opponent, ultimately crushing that team's will to fight.

Rockne emphasized over and over again, in public appearances, clinics, magazine articles, and in his "football class" at Notre Dame that this was "smart football." Combined with the intelligent use of the pass, which could be thrown by any of the running backs, the shift gave Rockne's Notre Dame teams an awesome, almost unstoppable offense. His teams won several games during his career in which only one touchdown was scored or the winning margin was the result of "perfect plays." The shift lingered as the characteristic Notre Dame approach to offensive football for more than a decade after Rockne' death. Although the T-formation ultimately replaced it, vestiges of the shift can be seen to this day in an offense where motion is prominent before the snap of the ball, or when a back shifts just prior to the snap (and rules changes designed to hamper Rockne's system keep modern football from ever looking exactly as he designed it).

This type of offensive strategy did not require what Rockne scathingly referred to as "bovine" or "elephantine" players. Instead, he demanded brains and speed. Many of his teams averaged under 180 pounds in the line, which may be instructively contrasted to the prototypical players needed for the old mass-play style of game, such as Yale's Pudge Heffelfinger at 6' 2", 230 pounds at the guard position, or Michigan's Germany Schulz at 6' 4", 240 at center. Indeed, the Irish had a starting center named John Eggeman who played from 1897-1899 at 6' 4", 256 pounds. Rockne's last teams featured what came to be known as "watch charm guards"—an image best captured in the diminutive Bert Metzger, the starting right guard on the 1930 National Champs who patrolled the line at 5' 9", 149 pounds and made first-team All-American on both the AP and UPI squads.

Eventually, the rules makers would whittle away at the shift, and its effectiveness, until, near the end of his career, Rockne was using a much heavier backfield. (See the Four Horsemen in 1924 at 162 pounds on average, versus the 1930 backfield, 20 pounds heavier per man ... in both cases, Rockne won the national title). Nevertheless, before the shift was legislated into oblivion, Rockne's methods allowed players of average size to become starting players in intercollegiate football for a period of fifteen or more years.

In this fashion, Rockne served his coaching apprenticeship under Harper for four years, 1914-1917. At the end of this period, Rockne was ready to leave Notre Dame and take a coaching position with the Michigan Aggies, now the Spartans of Michigan State. He was confident that his skills and methods had matured, and he needed security for a growing family—a motivation that accounted for several initiatives or moves he pondered or threatened in future years. As we know, Rockne's career would be spent at Notre Dame in its entirety, but he had several flings with other schools—USC, Iowa, and Columbia to mention the prominent ones. He learned to use the threat of leaving the Dome as leverage in his various negotiations with the university's administration and faculty, although it did not always work to his satisfaction. Eventually, he seems to have resigned himself to his position at Notre Dame, especially after his well-publicized affair with a signed contract to coach at Columbia. But he also seems to have compensated somewhat by throwing himself into numerous income-enhancing opportunities. In any case, after several years learning his coaching craft under Harper, he was ready to move on.

But Jesse Harper unexpectedly lost a relative in Kansas. He felt an obligation to leave coaching and look after a fairly large family ranch in that state. He recommended Rockne as his replacement and few were surprised that his wish was honored. Thus, seven years after arriving at the Notre Dame campus—apparently with some personal doubts and reservations at the time—Knute Rockne was positioned to have an opportunity that would launch him into the nation's consciousness as few have ever experienced it.

A stately Knure Rockne.

Rockne may have been personally prepared for his new position, but factors far beyond his control were threatening to make it a difficult situation. Since 1917, World War I had been wreaking havoc on college athletics. Athletes were prime candidates for military service. Players were leaving school to volunteer, or to enjoy some free

Rockne's first team as a head coach—the 1918 Irish.

Outstanding halfback
Jim Thorpe.

time before the inevitable call up, or were actually spending time in some form of military training. The 1918 season, Rockne's first as head coach, would be all but cancelled due to the influenza pandemic, partially as a result of American soldiers on troop ships that had previously carried infected swine—nearly perfect incubation conditions for a major disaster.

In the midst of this growing gloom, even before Harper had resigned, Rockne had encountered one of the most significant people he would ever deal with in his football career. He had met George Gipp.

The panoramic history of American sport, at least that which took root after Columbus initiated contact between European culture and the indigenous cultures in this hemisphere, is a relatively brief one. Organized sports—intercollegiate football, professional baseball—were only about fifty years in the making in 1920. There were genuine stars in the American sports pantheon by then: Christy Matthewson, Ty Cobb, Pudge Heffelfinger, Frank Hinkle, Jim Thorpe, John L. Sullivan, and Walter Johnson, to name a few. Great stories were and still are told about these superlative athletes. An American mythology of sports was already developing. The romance of sports was deeply felt by a large proportion of the American public. Rockne himself had already helped create some of the lore that sport thrives on ... and he would create much more as the decade of the 1920s wore on. This he would do in actual deeds but also in his countless reiterations of football stories, most of which make it difficult to separate fact from fancy from pure fiction. His own death in a tragic airplane accident would make him America's first martyr of sports. But there is probably nothing in this brief but impressive history of American sport, real or mythological, that quite compares with the Rockne-Gipp relationship. It contains all the action, melodrama, guile, emotion, humor, pathos, and sheer romanticism that any age could possibly desire. These things are invariably difficult to measure and prove, but it is highly likely that no single sports story exists that has surpassed it in its total impact on the American sports culture. It contains elements that are virtually universal, almost archetypal—the directionless young man who finds a mentor, numerous heroic exploits and tests in physical contests, a personality trying in quiet desperation to find meaning, sheer folly, clashes and difficulties between student and coach, a fall from grace, and a tragic early death.

George Gipp, like Knute Rockne, was already a grown man, at least physically, when he enrolled at Notre Dame. Unlike Rockne's, Gipp's life up to that point had not shown a great deal of promise outside of a certain facility in card sharking, pool hustling, and playing in YMCA basketball leagues. He never played baseball or football for his high school in Calumet, Michigan. He was usually ineligible because of his grades. After high school graduation in 1914, he worked construction and drove taxis. There was truly very little or no direction to

his life, certainly none of the spark of enthusiasm and drive that character-
ized the same period in Rockne's life. He did manage, however, to compile
some impressive statistics and a good reputation as an amateur baseball player
after high school. As Patrick Chelland's fine book on Gipp reveals, his emerging reputation in amateur baseball led a former Notre Dame baseball player,
Dolly Gray, to suggest that Gipp go to Notre Dame on a baseball scholarship. The situation was grim enough that Gipp's brother had to borrow the
train fare to send George to South Bend.

Like Rockne, Gipp was assigned to a room in Brownson Hall upon
arriving in the fall of 1916. Somehow, it does not seem likely that Gipp
would have had the kind of feelings for the nearby, looming Golden Dome
that Rockne seems to have harbored. In any case, Gipp's tenure at Brownson
was not a long one, as we shall see. Nevertheless, he also tried out, as Rockne
had, for the Brownson inter-hall football team, an ordeal which he managed
to endure for precisely one practice before quitting without explanation.
Chelland's biography of Gipp quotes a letter from Gipp to a friend written
shortly after arriving on the Notre Dame campus. In this, he admits that he
wondered what he was doing in college (given Gipp's social proclivities and
the austere atmosphere of the university, he has a good point here). He
admits to feeling a recurring kind of complaint. He confessed, in poignant,
self-conscious terms, that he felt "all wrong and will stay that way. ... I'd like
to give up ... chuck everything and go anywhere. ... Now I know that I'm

One of football's eternals—
George Gipp.

unlucky." Gipp would show a fairly strong quitter's syndrome, especially in varsity basketball and baseball as well
as his academic work at Notre Dame. He was not particularly well liked; he seemed aloof and cocksure. He seems
to have been a fairly typical young man, somewhat at loose ends, unchallenged, almost painfully shy, diffident to
an extreme, lacking direction, but blessed with native intelligence and athletic skills that had enjoyed no opportunity for public display and appreciation. In his posed photos, Gipp seems a bit uncomfortable—perhaps with
himself, surely with the situation of being on public display for the camera. In sum, on the surface he seems to be
a great example of the typical kind of motivational mystery often faced by most coaches. But there were depths to
the man—and whatever moved him—that were not apparent on the surface.

The story of how Rockne met Gipp has been immortalized in print and on film. Typically, Rockne did not
err in evaluating an athlete. Just as typically, Gipp was not impressed or excited. As the story goes, Rockne espied
him on a fall day in 1916. Or, more likely, he first saw a football soaring to a ridiculous height. The coach was
strolling across campus on his way to football practice and absent-mindedly watching some students who were
kicking footballs. He watched as one of them, a bit taller than the others and in street clothes, kicked to someone

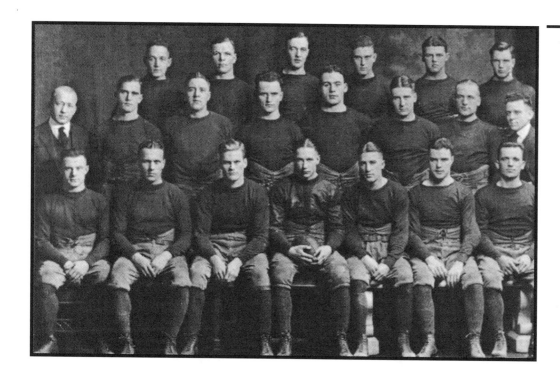

The undefeated 1919 Irish.

else more appropriately dressed in football gear, as Rockne recalled it, in "nothing more than a casual duet of punts." Shocked, Rockne saw that the tall student was casually drop-kicking the ball with ease and grace—for fifty yards and more! Rockne, accustomed to the hero worship accorded a coach by students, promptly asked for the young man's name. He received a reply characteristic of Gipp's general indifference to the scene around him. After a perfunctory introduction, Rockne then invited Gipp to try out for the freshman team. Gipp did so and, according to legend, immediately showed his mettle on his first play from scrimmage by slashing through the freshmen's defense for a long touchdown. It sounds like the kind of thing that ends up in the reject pile or on the cutting room floor, but it was the beginning of an unforgettable and sometimes painful chapter in Rockne's real life.

Gipp's exploits as a Notre Dame star—and problem child—began in his first freshman game, against Western State Normal (now Western Michigan) when, having been directed by the quarterback to punt, he instead drop-kicked a field goal to win the game—from his own thirty-eight-yard line. This feat, resulting in a 62-yard field goal, surely must stand as one of the longest on record in collegiate football history (ND's official longest varsity field goal was booted in 1976 by Dave Reeve: 53 yards). Other standout performances involving Gipp include his game-winning touchdown against Indiana in 1920, a goal line smash accomplished while he had a dislocated shoulder (motivated, it seems, by a bet, according to Murray Sperber), and his entire athletic exhibition against a tough Army team in 1920. His efforts in this latter game, against one of the best teams in the country, are still impressive: 20 carries for 150 yards, 5 completed passes in 9 attempts for another 123 yards, and 207 additional yards gained on 2 punt returns and 8 kickoff returns. In a single game, Gipp had produced the staggering figure of 480 yards of all-purpose offense. His heroic performance led the exasperated Army coach to assert, "Gipp is no football player … he's a runaway sonofabitch." The Army coaches and players would not have found it much more amusing to learn that Gipp had also bet $400 on the game.

George Gipp and Paul Castner on the left in 1920 action against Nebraska.

In his 26 varsity football games for Notre Dame, Gipp rushed for 100 yards on 10 occasions. In 1920, he rushed 102 times for 827 yards and an amazing 8.1 yards per carry. In those 26 games, Gipp's total yardage (rushes, completed passes, receptions, runbacks) came to 4,833 yards—for a stunning 185 yards produced every time he stepped on a football field. The offensive production was handled along with his duties as a defensive back and all-purpose kicker, facts that modern record holders for offense cannot claim. Rockne summed up Gipp's efforts as a defensive back by asserting that a forward pass was never completed in territory defended by Gipp— the usual Rockne hyperbole, but probably with a core of truth to it.

A further measure of the heroic stature of Gipp's athletic prowess can be found in his stats Chelland cites for summer league amateur baseball. In the summer of 1919, he batted .494 with 12 home runs in only 83 at bats, with 33 runs scored. In the 1920 summer season, Gipp played in 14 games; he stole 6 bases and batted .375 (18 for 48), with 3 doubles, 3 triples, and 3 homers.

These remarkable statistics from two sports clearly show Gipp to have been everything that a sports hero could be in the realm of competition. But there was another side to George Gipp, the side that compelled him to live alone in the Oliver Hotel in downtown South Bend after his first year at Notre Dame. There he was free of the rigorous discipline (the parietals) that governed on-campus residents. He could drink and play pool and cards in marathon contests without worrying about the obvious recriminations. In this way, he seems to have found a happy compromise between the demands of college life and the life he really wanted to live, one perhaps related to the desire he stated in his wistful 1916 letter—"to chuck everything and go anywhere." He could respond magnificently to a competitive challenge and defeat a gaggle of opponents; he could function superbly and instinctively as a leader in a team game. Nevertheless, at bottom, Gipp was a loner, almost a recluse. The one constant in his life seems to have been the need for a competitive challenge of some sort—a need which Rockne surely recognized and with which he must have empathized. The questions for Rockne had to revolve around these issues: [1] if Gipp needs competition, how can this best be steered into intercollegiate athletics and not squandered on all-night poker sessions at the Oliver Hotel? [2] How best to keep Gipp somehow remotely close to the academic track without attracting too much attention ... in other words, how to maintain at least a facade of academic respectability? [3] How to do [1] and [2] without alienating the other players on the team or in some adverse way, destroying team morale and harmony?

Naively perhaps, or maybe even a touch cynically, the coach asserted that Gipp led a quiet life with few friends, cared little for women, and seldom studied (note the unstated agenda here of avoiding "distractions"). All in all, Rockne thought that Gipp was less afflicted than most by "the usual faults" of star performers. Be that as it may, Gipp lived and acted with a certain breathtaking disregard or disdain for accepted norms. In football practice, where Rockne's keen eye surely noticed divergent behavior, as Chelland shows, Gipp was seldom on time. In 1917, he was three weeks late showing up for classes; in 1918, he did not bother to take his final examinations. In 1919, the day after beating Purdue, he joined some other Irish players to play for pay in a semi-pro game in Rockford, Illinois. Murray Sperber reports that Gipp's academic transcript for the entire 1918-1919 school year is blank—he received no grades in all of his subjects. (Why not? He didn't bother to take the final exams). On other occasions, a Notre Dame student living off campus reported seeing Rockne escorting Gipp from South Bend to the university, apparently in an effort to get him to class and keep him academically eligible for football. The towns-people of South Bend—or anyone who frequented the Oliver Hotel or Hullie & Mike's pool hall or the surrounding streets—would have had ample opportunity to see Gipp in less than sober condition.

Then there is the matter of the infamous "oral exam" supposedly taken by Gipp in the spring of 1920 to regain admission to the university after being expelled. In Rockne's 1930 account in his *Autobiography*, he took great care to put the best face possible on the whole lamentable affair. He noted that Gipp had been expelled for

Hullie and Mike's,
a Gipp hangout.

missing too many classes, but that he urged his erstwhile star to make up the work. According to Rockne, Gipp asked if an oral examination could be arranged. He claimed illness as an excuse for the class cuts. The exam was reportedly arranged. To conclude, Rockne claimed Gipp amazed everybody involved in the exam with his command of the material. Gipp passed and seemingly learned his lesson, for his attendance then became regular.

Chelland and Sperber identify Rockne's story as pure fiction. Gipp had been, in fact, expelled on March 8 by university President Burns. Apparently unfazed by this turn of events, Gipp used his considerable spare time to hustle pool and partake of other games of chance for six weeks. Other schools made serious pitches for Gipp's football services. Outraged local citizens bent the president's ear. A petition was sent to Father Burns by prominent South Bend citizens, and that apparently turned the trick, so to speak. He readmitted Gipp on April 29, 1920. Before long, Gipp was playing baseball for the Irish, having made a smooth transition from the billiards green to the green of the diamond.

Did Rockne fail to distinguish between fact and fiction here? He consistently showed a cavalier disregard for what must be called historical accuracy. In less significant cases than Gipp's, he seems to have had a collection of cut and paste, mix and match story components that could be woven in different ways into a basic story line. This could have been a simple coping skill for dealing with the constant demands of the press and an adoring public. Surely, it would not be surprising if Rockne attempted to preserve his own public image. He was culpable to a degree in Gipp's academic abuse; he had, after all, more or less turned a blind eye to Gipp's antics. It would be surprising if he had nothing to do with the pressure applied from South Bend.

Rockne, by 1930, had been at Notre Dame for two decades. While he had built a small athletic empire, he surely must have been made aware of the school's demand for integrity. In some ways, Rockne was trapped between the desire to protect the image of George Gipp, which Rockne had largely created, and the need to meet the university's expectations for integrity. All of his accounts of Gipp tend to minimize, overlook, or ignore the less illustrious aspects of Gipp's life. He seems to have attempted to create the man and player he wished had been. For instance, Rockne claimed that Gipp's father was a minister, which was not true.

The nature of the relationship between Rockne and Gipp, both in life and after Gipp's premature death in 1920, indicates that Rockne felt an unusual bond, a sense of spiritual kinship with his wayward wonder. His chapter on Gipp in his *Autobiography* states, "Gipp was nature's pet and, as with many of her pets, she also punished him." He concluded his remarks with adulation: "A boy does well indeed who, so young, leaves the clean glory of a name behind." Several thoughts come to mind here—nature presented in a maternal image, operating as a punitive agent. Rockne had complete disdain for what he saw as effeminate distractions. Recall that he took note of what he considered to be the fact that Gipp did not have a female in his life (even though it would be hard to see residency in the Oliver Hotel for four years as monastic and celibate). Rockne, the only male child in a family of five children, seems to have constructed an adult life that was almost completely devoid of females in terms of those compelling athletic activities he threw himself into … even though he worked at a university dedicated to Our Lady. In essence, the world Rockne constructed for himself was a male bastion, both literally and figuratively;

women—and female principles in general—could be seen as a threat to this male domain. The comment that Gipp was punished by a female Nature is thus revealing of a set of important attitudes held by Rockne.

Another thought regarding this is the direct reference to the "clean glory of a name [left] behind" the lost star. Glory was definitely a part of Gipp's brief, meteoric public career, but the underlying reality was not exactly "clean." Perhaps times have changed enough that Gipp's extracurricular activities do not seem highly irregular or outlandish, but I think not. First of all, he would not today have any chance whatsoever of playing intercollegiate sports with his meager academic qualifications and collegiate record. Players currently often have two or three games completed before the rest of the student body appears on campus, a pattern that reverses Gipp's missing three weeks in 1917. Secondly, his living arrangements would have been monitored much more rigorously than in 1917-1920. To make a living with gambling skills would today be scandalous in the highest degree, easily the kind of transgression that could end a collegiate career. Finally, from a pragmatic standpoint, few reputable coaches would have the patience to allow a player to abuse the most basic team rules, or maintain a pattern of favoritism over several seasons, without earning the justifiable enmity of many players on the team.

That Rockne managed to pull all this off is a measurement, to be sure, of social and ethical changes that have occurred since his era. But it also reveals intriguing facets of Rockne the coach as well as the state of affairs

Undefeated for a second consecutive year, the 1920 Irish. Gipp's photo was pasted in after his death.

surrounding collegiate football of that time. Regarding Rockne, it reveals a coach very much in control of the scene around him, even if that control included harboring and protecting a player on the verge of being uncontrollable. One wonders if the coach would have coddled this player this way in 1930 rather than 1920. Gipp's varsity years coincided with Rockne's first three years as head coach; surely Rockne was doing what he could to consolidate the various elements of his new domain. He might not have had complete confidence in his own management skills. We surely see early evidence in the whole Gipp affair that Notre Dame football was taking on a seemingly independent dimension within the university community, an issue (whether true or not) that has been controversial within the various factions of that community, not the least being a significant portion of the faculty.

These are imponderables. Part of the innate intrigue and attractiveness of this story in Rockne's life is the number of sheer unknowns. In the vacuum of information and facts, people have a fine opportunity to see what they want to see. Still, it may be said that Rockne's greatest single player possessed many attributes that Rockne must have admired or even desired—especially Gipp's tremendous, uncanny, and largely unexploited physical gifts (and a matching diffidence about them). Gipp was a natural athlete and, it seems, a quietly competent team leader … some sort of authority emanated from him, even if it was only supreme confidence when facing an athletic challenge. (This confidence does not appear to have been present in other pursuits). Rockne, on the contrary, had trained himself mercilessly and doggedly to be able to compete against gifted athletes like Gipp. Furthermore, Rockne must have made a tremendous effort to overcome his own shyness. Gipp did not seem to care about much; Rockne burned with an intensity entirely alien to Gipp's life. The coach seems to have spent the better part of a decade creating and then preserving his own image of the player. Doing so may have been some kind of deeply internalized mandate.

George Gipp died on December 14, 1920, at the age of twenty-five. His last season at Notre Dame had been a brilliant tribute to his football prowess. He overcame various kinds of physical adversity all through the season. Chelland's book notes that Dr. A. C. Roche of Calumet advised Gipp to have his chronically infected tonsils surgically removed before going into the 1920 football season. Gipp ignored the advice.

Following his splendid effort in the Army game on October 30, one of the Cadets reported seeing Gipp in the shower and was amazed by the star's "emaciated" condition. Two weeks later, on November 13, Gipp dislocated his shoulder in the Indiana game. Rather than return to South Bend, Gipp went to Chicago to redeem a promise to a coaching friend to demonstrate the art of drop-kicking to some high school players. He apparently either caught or aggravated a cold during the demonstration, which took place on a bone-chilling day, when the Chicago temperatures were in the 20° range. The next game was with Northwestern in Chicago on November 20 and was heralded by local Notre Dame alumni clubs as "George Gipp Day."

Rockne followed his usual practice of not revealing players' illnesses or injuries to the press. Gipp did not start the game. The crowd of 20,000 chanted Gipp's name for more than three quarters. Although he had warmed up with some kicks before the game, he subsequently stood along the sidelines on that cold Chicago day for more than two hours, possibly risking hypothermia, as Joe Montana did in the 1979 Cotton Bowl (and he had started the whole first half of that game). In any case, Rockne relented and sent Gipp into the game in the fourth quarter. He threw 6 passes, completing 5 of them, with two going for TDs of 35 and 70 yards. He also attempted to return a punt, but was unable to function effectively in his exhausted condition. Game accounts in the Chicago press reveal that Northwestern's downfield players, in good positions to tackle Gipp, refused to drill him in his weakened condition but instead gently brought him to a stop. After the game, Gipp suffered chills and began to run a high temperature. On Tuesday, November 23, he had to excuse himself from the team's annual banquet, due

The dinner program from the 1920 team banquet.

to illness, and, with Rockne's help, checked into St. Joseph's Hospital in South Bend early the next morning.

Gipp never left the hospital. The campus and nation waited for three weeks for the daily bulletins on his medical condition. Without him, on November 25, Notre Dame played and defeated Michigan State by a score of 25-0. Meanwhile, Gipp's cold and chronic tonsillitis led to pneumonia. He died of a systemic infection, streptococcal hemolytic septeropymia, according to Patrick Chelland's account. Rockne's longtime friend, Francis Wallace, recorded that Gipp weighed a pitiful eighty pounds when he died. Given these facts, a physician friend, Dr. M. J. Lane, once told me that it would be virtually impossible to second guess Rockne's decision to send Gipp into the closing moments of the Northwestern game.

According to Rockne, as Gipp neared death, he said, "Some time, Rock, when the team's up against it, when things are wrong and the breaks are beating the boys—tell them to go in there with all they've got and win just one for the Gipper. I don't know where I'll be then, Rock. But I'll know about it, and I'll be happy." This is the famous supposed request that Rockne shared with his 1928 team as it struggled against a superior Army team.

Near the end of their rich lives, I interviewed two of Gipp's teammates, Paul Castner (the fullback, a man who also played with the famous Four Horsemen two years later) and Chet Grant, a quarterback, whose familiarity with Notre Dame football long preceded both Rockne and Gipp. Both differed with the details of Rockne's account of this central event in American sports mythology. Castner believed that Gipp was entirely capable of making such a request and that it was typical of Rockne to have used it later at the right psychological moment. Both men admitted that no one will ever know the full truth. But one thing is certain, they told me, and that is that Gipp never referred to himself as "the Gipper." They believed that it was possible that something had happened between Rockne and Gipp that fateful December day in the South Bend hospital. They agreed that it is possible that something like the quotation represented by Rockne was uttered by Gipp. It is probable, then, that Rockne's active imagination simply recalled the thrust of the conversation and not the minute particulars. It is also possible, in my view, that Rockne basically invented the entire episode whole cloth and used it when it best suited him. These were, after all, supposedly among the last words a dying man said to his coach. Rockne was filled with good stories; he was a public figure, one with a gift for the well-turned phrase. He talked sports anywhere and everywhere. We know that he was entirely capable of inventing situations to suit his purposes when it came to football. In the eight years that had passed from the time of Gipp's death until the 1928 Army game (if Gipp really said this), Rockne must have given much thought to the incident, biding his time for the correct moment to employ it. In the final analysis, perhaps the best that can be said of the famous exhortation—"Win One for the Gipper!"—is that it might have a general basis in fact but that it's likely that Gipp never said it in so many words. And there is the possibility that Gipp never said it at all.

That Rockne's rhetoric produced a galvanizing effect on an underachieving, overmatched team—that it immediately caught the public's fancy and then entered the cultural mainstream—is a measure of Rockne's unique genius in motivational matters. Rockne loved the inherent dramatic value that football displayed. In this famous instance, he may have outperformed himself.

When Rockne took over the head coaching duties of the 1918 Irish, the war had already had caused a significant impact on the collegiate athletic scene, with many of the best athletes ticketed for the service. He had a pretty good core of players, but it was small: Gipp, to be sure, Hunk Anderson, Clipper Smith, Eddie Anderson, Pete Bahan, Norm Barry, and a young fullback named Curly Lambeau—who would score the first touchdown of the Rockne era in the opener against Case Tech, setting up a set of intriguing resonances between Notre Dame football and a small town in Wisconsin, Green Bay, that would continue for half a century. Notre Dame won the game 26-6, Gipp playing a solid game, then the team sat around for a month before the next contest as two games with military teams were canceled due to the influenza epidemic. Many practices were also canceled, leaving only the frosh team for the varsity to compete against with government permission. After a month, on a Friday night, the Irish were told that they had permission to play Wabash the next day. Releasing pent-up frustrations, they hammered the Little Giants 67-7. Gipp had his second 100-yard rushing game, with Bahan, Gipp, and Lambeau all scoring two TDs each. A week later, the Irish tied a Great Lakes service team 7-7; Gipp missed a field goal that would have won the game. The collegians were, on paper, outclassed by the likes of George Halas and Paddy O'Driscoll, but Rockne turned

Paul Castner, one of four Irish players to have played both with Gipp and the Four Horsemen.

in a sparkling coaching performance. Even his guile, however, could not overcome a total quagmire in the next game as ND fell to the Michigan Aggies 13-7; Gipp's services were limited by a broken blood vessel in his face. Purdue was next and they fell 26-6, with Gipp dominating the game with his running (19 carries for 137 yards), passing, kicking, and defense. The season ended with a frustrating 0-0 tie with Nebraska, although the Irish had their chances. But the refs were a factor, with two calls overturning a score and then a drive to the Husker 8 yard line. Nebraska never earned a first down. With that final indignity, a frustrating initial season came to an end with a 3-1-2 record. Rockne had to have felt some satisfaction in that his team was never really out of any game. The two ties could have been wins with a bit more luck. Rockne could breathe a bit easier knowing that he'd surely never again see another such list of adverse conditions.

Roger Kiley, two-year starter at end for Rockne.

The 1919 Irish squad must have been a pleasing sight to the coach because a strong contingent of returning vets from the 1916 team would join Gipp, the Andersons, and Bahan to create a powerhouse. Much like the Irish under Leahy after World War Two with their four consecutive undefeated campaigns, this group and new recruits would go undefeated for two seasons, and compile a 28-1 record over three seasons. Notre Dame started out modestly enough, with a 14-0 win over Kalamazoo; Gipp rushed for 148 yards and had two long TDs predictably called back by the referees. Mt. Union, of Ohio, fell next, a bevy of backs scoring in a 60-7 rout. Gipp had his usual four-dimensional game. Rockne let Gipp keep up that kind of pace in a 14-9 victory over archrival Nebraska, but his passing (5 of 8 for completions, for 124 yards) was the difference in the game, stats that don't count a lateral from him to Dutch Bergman that resulted in a 90-yard TD run. Notre Dame next walloped Western Michigan, 53-0, with Gipp leading the starters with two TDs; the subs did the rest. Rockne decided to rest his starters some in the Indiana game, saving them for Army, although Gipp had modest running and passing yards plus a drop-kicked field goal in a 16-3 win. There wasn't quite enough rest for Bergman though; he hurt a knee and missed the Army game. Gipp had to make up the difference, running for 70 yards and passing for 115 more. Rockne had to be pleased with a defensive effort that stopped the Cadets several times at or near the Irish 5, to preserve a 12-9 win. After that, ND had to face the Michigan Aggies, losers earlier to Western Michigan. Maybe they relaxed, or let the Aggies' 50-piece marching band distract them, but the Irish won a close game, 13-0. Gipp had two interceptions; Rockne had to resort to using a tackle eligible play for the game's clinching score. The Irish let Purdue score first, then drubbed them for a 33-13 win ... Gipp fired two TD passes as he completed 11 of 15 throws for 217 yards. Rockne's team closed out the season undefeated with a 14-6 win over Morningside. Gipp scored the TDs and ended a Morningside drive with an interception. In what amounted to Rockne's first complete season (since much of the '18 campaign had been canceled), the Irish stood atop the western schools. Harvard, at 9-0-1, was the only major power that had a comparable record.

The 1920 season would be memorable on several counts ... a second consecutive undefeated season, stirring wins over major opponents, Rockne's first consensus All-American in George Gipp, and then the tragic death of Gipp at age 25. It all started with a 39-0 victory over Kalamazoo; Gipp had his best game as a Notre Dame runner with 183 yards on 16 carries. Western Normal (now Western Michigan) next folded, 42-0, even though Rockne's charges had three TDs called back for penalties. A tough Nebraska team stymied most of the Irish in ND's 16-7 win, holding thm to 174 total yards, but Gipp was torrid—managing the interesting statistical feat of gaining 218 total yards, 44 yards more than the Irish team total. Valparaiso toppled next, 28-3 ... a game that stands out because Rockne here tested his notion of using what he called the "shock troops" (apparently borrowed from World War I tactics). He started the game with subs (with one caveat—they needed a good punter to keep them out of deep trouble). The starters, meanwhile, could observe the opposition ... and build up their motivation to get into the game. Not surprisingly, Rockne seems to have liked the inherent suspense provided by this little mystery play. When the starters came into the game, the opposition was in for some trouble. So, Valparaiso kicked a field goal for a 3-0 lead, and even snagged a Gipp pass once the starters were in for good, but Gipp scored twice and otherwise made himself a nuisance as the Irish went on to a 28-3 win. Army was undefeated and banged the Irish around for a 17-14 halftime lead, but the Irish kept steady pressure on the Cadets in the second half for a 27-17 win. Gipp had one of the best games an Irish back has ever had: 150 yards rushing, 5 of 9 passes completed for 123 yards and a TD, 129 yards for 3 punts, and 207 yards on various kick returns. Rockne may have had some concerns about his star after this game; he tried to rest him a bit against Purdue, but Gipp ran amok anyway—with a 35-yard TD run, 129 yards running, 128 yards in completed passes, and 3 PAT kicks. No team from within Indiana had beaten ND since 1906, but the Hoosiers almost turned the trick, except that Gipp scored a TD with a dislocated shoulder to insure a 13-10 win. His hometown friend, Hunk Anderson, played the game with cracked ribs, no mean feat for an interior lineman (helping to earn Grantland Rice's respect as the toughest player he ever knew, pound for pound). Notre Dame next beat Northwestern 33-7 on the day billed as "George Gipp Day" by the ND alumni in Chicago. But Gipp was obviously ill; Rockne kept him out of the game until late ... and he struck for 157 yards on 5 pass completions, including TDs to Roger Kiley and Norm Barry. This game took place on November 20; three days later the team had its annual banquet ... at Gipp's old stomping grounds,

All-Americans from 1930: Marty Brill, Rockne's associate
Christy Walsh, and Frank Carideo.

the Oliver Hotel in South Bend. The star had to leave the festivities, though, ill enough to check in to a local hospital early in the morning. Three weeks after "George Gipp Day," in Chicago, he joined the ages. While he gamely fought against his fatal illness, his teammates beat the Michigan Aggies 25-0 to complete consecutive undefeated seasons. Sophomore fullback Paul Castner led the way with two TDs. Gipp earned consensus All-American honors; Roger Kiley also snagged some All-American attention. And the world may never come to know whatever the dying Gipp said, or didn't say, to his coach.

The 1920 season confirmed Rockne's promise as a coach. He was no flash in the pan. He was no longer dealing almost entirely with holdover players from the Harper years. He could recruit with the best of them, develop intriguing game strategies, assess personnel wisely, motivate players perhaps better than all of his peers, and exploit his team's strengths and an opponent's weaknesses ruthlessly. He may also have learned well the wisdom of being wary of what you pray for—you may actually have your prayers answered.

It must be noted that the hectic years that Rockne spent with Gipp as a dominant player and personality altered his way of building a team. He never again fielded a team in which a single player dominated to the extent that Gipp had in his era. The backfield that became known as the Four Horsemen was, in 1923 and 1924, a supreme blend of individual skills. The brilliant Marchmont Schwartz of the 1930 team was complemented by the heady Frank Carideo, powerful Joe Savoldi, and speedy Marty Brill—a group often called Rockne's second Four Horsemen. Two-time All-American Christy Flanagan led the team in rushing for the three seasons following the Four Horsemen, but his skills were clearly subordinated to the intricate demands of the teamwork necessary to execute the Notre Dame shift. Gipp also played in the shift system, but, unlike later players, seemed to have a flair for inventing plays. A case in point, but one of many, is the 1919 Kalamazoo game in which Gipp reportedly freelanced a brilliant play when he realized he was trapped behind the line of scrimmage. This ad-lib play on his part was the first recorded running pass, according to Chelland.

Rockne had not recruited Gipp, not in the sense of having glowing reports come in from the hinterlands about some local star. In Gipp's case, there had been no high school star to promote to a college coach. He went to Notre Dame to play baseball, not football, based on amateur ball, rather than high school feats. Given what we know of his unimpressive academic habits and somewhat aimless extracurricular pursuits, Gipp had developed no goals or plans related to an academic background. College permitted him to compete at a high competitive level in fun ways, and did not seem to threaten his other revenue-producing interests. Via intercollegiate sports, college might actually promote his continuing to have competitive fun—allowing Gipp to be paid fairly well above the table. In some ways, he was an ideal player to work with, since Rockne did not seem to have to attend to Gipp's academics too much. In a strange way, Gipp made that part easy. . . though it's likely that the total package he provided drove Rockne to distraction on many occasions.

Even after Gipp's death, Rockne's name was not yet a household word. He was known in coaching circles, of course, but he had not developed into the spellbinding public speaker of later years, the syndicated writer, or the radio personality. He had not then chosen to take the Irish team from coast to coast for games as he would beginning in 1926. For the most part, Notre Dame's games had been played in the Midwest. In 1920, for instance, they played four homes games at Notre Dame, and one each in Indianapolis, Chicago, East Lansing, and Lincoln, Nebraska. Only one game was played outside the geographical boundaries of the Midwest, Army at West Point. Rockne recognized the relative limitations of such a provincial schedule and began to work on creating a more representative schedule, but it would take a few years to put the pieces together.

The Irish teams of the Gipp era were not yet a mass-consumption product. Stadiums had not grown to the point where crowds of more than 75,000 were common. The 1920 team played before a grand total of 85,000 people in its undefeated season (the renovated and enlarged football stadium at Notre Dame holds almost this many fans for one game today). With Rockne working hard to put Notre Dame on the fast track, they played before 197,000 in 1923 and, in 1926, before 350,000. In that season, the team made its first trip to the West Coast for a regularly scheduled game, where it defeated Southern California 13-12 in the new Los Angeles Coliseum before 75,000 fans—al-

The proud dad with Jack and Jeanne.

most as many people at this one game as the entire 1920 attendance figure. Unlike schedule making today, which is often done in advance by ten or twelve years, Rockne was able to make up a season's schedule only one year in advance. In this manner, he could try to schedule teams that provided Notre Dame the greatest publicity in each section of the country. As he took the team up against selected intersectional rivals (Georgia Tech was added in 1922), the Notre Dame team became known as "Rockne's Ramblers," an appellation that came to bother senior administrators at Notre Dame. As the crowds grew, as the team played more intersectional contests, and Rockne became a marketable entity in his own right in the media and from the podium, his fame grew proportionally. His increasing popularity was the best example of a gradual evolutionary process that had begun at the turn of the century, a process that saw the importance of the team's elected captain and graduate manager decline as the "professional" coaches rose to power. Within a period of twenty years or so, the team captain had dwindled from being the most important figure (such as ND's Red Salmon in 1903) to a pro forma, largely empty honor. If these developing patterns mean anything, it is that intercollegiate football was well into the take-off stage with regard to becoming institutionalized as mass entertainment. As a profitable extracurricular university-sponsored event, it had become too important for student athletes to operate alone. Rockne's increasing fame was intimately related to this burgeoning interest. Indeed, more than any other figure of this period, Rockne may be given credit for the game's increasingly widespread acceptance.

Gipp's tremendous career and tragic death provided the country with the chivalric, romantic martyr needed to sanctify the game. In all the sports writing and commentaries about football, there was a dominant metaphorical concern that described football as a religious, chivalric, martial event. With this in mind, it is important to see that Gipp's death became a larger event than it might have been under different circumstances.

The rise to prominence of Michigan, Chicago, and Notre Dame moved the balance of power away from the historical locus of the "Big Three" in the East (Harvard, Yale, and Princeton—an artificial dominance created largely by Walter Camp's geographical myopia) and placed it in the general direction of the Midwest. With this shift away from the East, the game was truly becoming national in its scope. In addition, with the focus of attention shifted away from the obsolete, closed style of play practiced in the East and so rudely exposed in the Irish win over Army in 1913, Rockne's philosophy of open football benefited from maximum exposure. By the time that this process of change was completed, radio had become an important medium for the game, and the popularity of the open, flashy brand of football had grown even more.

Rockne's open style of playing the game was far better designed for public consumption than was the archaic closed style of mass play. Rockne's teams executed flawlessly, but the major difference between the two kinds of approaches to the game as marketable products was that spectators could literally see the ball better in the open game. In the closed game, the backfield was drawn up tight to the offensive line, the center's snap was over a short distance, and the players, often without identifying numbers or differentiating uniforms, sort of smashed together in an unseemly heap. It was brutal and rather artless—a vestige of the banned flying wedge formations and tackle-backs tactics of the 1890 era that led to Teddy Roosevelt's concerns.

Rockne dispensed with all this. The shift as he developed it (via Harper) was devastatingly deceptive for a defender but allowed the spectator to see who carried the ball, the direction of the attack, and, if all worked well, running and passing plays that covered much greater territory per play than in the closed game (e.g., Gipp's amazing average of 8.1 yards per carry in the 1920 season). Additionally, Rockne introduced the idea of different colored uniforms for opposing teams after the disappointment of Notre Dame's only loss of the 1921 season, when Iowa won 10-7 partially because of their interception of an Irish pass attempt created by the confusing similarity of the teams' dark uniforms. Another improvement developed by Rockne was to replace canvas with satin material for the uniform pants. This allowed for a tighter fit, better-padded protection, less loose material for a would-be tackler to grab, and considerably more eye appeal for the spectator. The colorful spectacles provided in today's football games have their origins in Rockne's concern for the game's appeal to the spectator.

The 1921 season also witnessed the first of Rockne's "suicide schedules" in which several major teams

The 1921 Irish won ten and lost one.

were engaged (Iowa, Purdue, Nebraska, Indiana, Army, Rutgers, Michigan State) rather than a series of patsies pointing toward one or two important rivals. The 1920 season had seen his first use of "shock troops" to begin a game—his startling idea to begin a game with substitutes—which had tactical merit to be sure but also satisfied his dramatic purpose as a master showman, increasing the game's sense of climax when the beleaguered second unit would be "saved" by the sudden arrival of the first string (a tactic partially conditioned by the conservative substitution rules then in effect). This tactic paved the way for the subsequent rules changes that allowed for two-platoon football and, ultimately, perhaps, the modern use of specialists—players who perform one task exclusively—which Rockne would use wisely in a 1928 game with Army.

The football commentators and arbiters of the day, such as Walter Camp and John Heisman, revealed an organic sense of the development of the game. These figures made it clear that there were important, ongoing changes, usually related to the pass and later to the shift, as well as a gradual evolution of tactics based on an increased understanding of the potential complexity of the game. Other improvements included better execution of the game's basic features—blocking, pass defense, kicking, and the like. Rockne's ideas and teams were central features in this development of football.

Chet Wynne, Irish fullback
on three Gipp teams.

Rockne's everlasting fame became assured in the fall of 1921, when the players who later came to be known as the Four Horsemen (not to mention the Seven Mules) enrolled at Notre Dame. The four backfield men, who in 1921 had little to recommend them as future sports immortals, were reincarnated by Grantland Rice on October 19, 1924. Much went into this final act in the process of making Rockne the most famous football figure in the country. It required, first, that Notre Dame and Rockne come to be associated together, second, that the Four Horsemen exist as mere mortals before Rice penned his description of the 1924 Army game, and, third, that there be a national consciousness that was emotionally, socially, and culturally prepared to worship these seemingly apocalyptic figures.

But all that was merely in the offing; Rockne had to get on with the project in the form of the 1921 season. If there was ever a good reason to move to a stronger schedule, Kalamazoo provided it in the opener: Chet Wynne basically won the game with an 80-yard TD run with the opening kickoff. The Irish backfield had a field day. The fifth-string QB, Frank Reese, even scored twice (one was nullified by a penalty). Kalamazoo completed its first pass in the third quarter...for a loss. The Irish intercepted more passes than Kalamazoo completed on the way to a 56-0 mismatch win. A second patsy, DePauw, went down 57-10; Wynne and John Mohardt both scored four TDs each. The winning-streak bubble burst, after 22 games without a loss since the 1918 season, when Iowa pulled off a 10-7 upset

win. The Irish dominated in all phases of the game: 456 total yards to Iowa's 216; 239 yards rushing to 216 (much more, though, than Rockne-led defenses usually surrendered); 227 yards passing to Iowa's 10 (!!); 22 first downs to 14. But Irish penalties aided the Hawkeyes' first scoring drive, early in the game, and a field goal followed not long after. Notre Dame played catch-up after that and never pulled it off. Castner just missed a 50-yard field goal that would have averted the loss.

The Irish had to pick up the pieces and get on with the season. Purdue fell to an aroused Notre Dame squad 33-0. Guard Hunk Anderon, of all people, led a 30-0 blitz in the first half by scoring two TDs within a three-minute period—via a blocked punt and then a fumbled punt. After that, Nebraska found hope for a vulnerable Irish team in the Iowa loss, but ND prevailed 7-0, John Mohardt scoring the game's only TD on a run shortly after a bad Husker punt. Next, the Irish knocked off Indiana 28-7, with Castner scoring a TD and leading an aroused defense with three interceptions near the end of the game. In their last three games, the Irish defense had given up a total of 10 first downs.

The end of the 1921 season came about in an odd way—four games played in 14 days—On Saturday, November 5, the Irish defeated Army 28-0. On Tuesday, November 8, ND blasted Rutgers 48-0, Castner leading the way with two TDs and two field goals. The next Saturday, Haskell succumbed 42-7; Castner scored three TDs. The starters played about four minutes...while Rockne scouted Marquette. In one week, the Irish had won three games by a combined score of 118-7. Marquette

Halfback John Mohardt.

proved to be a different matter; they scored first, following a block of a Castner punt. Then Mohardt took command—scoring on a 48-yard run, passing 45 yards to Eddie Anderson for another, and setting up Chet Wynne's TD with a 35-yard jaunt. The Michigan Aggies folded in the finale 48-0, with the Irish center, Harry Mehre, starting the scoring with a runback of an interception.

Six of Rockne's charges earned All-American accolades for their 1921 season's labors (Kiley, Eddie and Hunk Anderson, Mohardt, Castner, Buck Shaw). The Rose Bowl showed some interest in inviting the Irish, but Rockne knew that several key players had been caught playing in a semi-pro game and he did not press the matter.

The 1922 Irish squad would be the first of Rockne's entire making. He had some carry over players from the Harper years, most notably Gipp, into 1921. But this was his team entirely now. Guard Hunk Anderson had graduated, a major loss. He had only one starter from the '21 backfield, all-purpose fullback Paul Castner. Youngsters would have to step up. Rockne had noticed a bright frosh prospect in quarterback Harry Stuhldreher, who had the kind of personal qualities reminiscent of Rockne's hero from his youth, Walter Eckersall. He did well enough to operate as the number two quarterback while his classmates, Elmer Layden and Don Miller (of a family that would have players at ND over four decades), would round out the backfield.

Kalamazoo was still the opening sacrifice and they fared little better than in the past. The Irish pasted

The 1922 Irish had the fledgling Horsemen as sophomores.

them 46-0, simply outmanning them. Castner took a kickoff back for 95 yards; Miller duplicated the feat and tacked on TD runs of 30 and 14 yards. St. Louis next fell, 26-0. Rockne's defense looked solid after two games; he decreased the backfield combinations and began to point the team toward the more difficult games. His young runners showed him that they were beginning to get the hang of the shift's intricacies. Purdue was the next opponent, always a dangerous team for ND. The Boilermakers put up good resistance, but succumbed 20-0, ND's third consecutive shutout. The Irish suffered a considerable loss when starting tackle Tom Lieb broke a leg in this game. DePauw broke the string of shotouts but lost anyway, 34-7.

In a move that previewed today's football played in domed stadiums, Rockne had the Irish practice for Georgia Tech amid howling noises, trying to prepare the squad for the famous Rebel Yell that the Tech followers were sure to use. He also used a fake illness for one of his children as a motivational ploy before the game. The Irish shock troops fell behind 3-0 so Rockne hustled in the starters, but Tech was a grudging opponent. Stuhldreher led a careful drive, capped by a TD pass to Castner. Much of the rest of the game was a defensive stalemate, the outcome in doubt, until a Tech mistake in special teams gave ND good field position ... Stuhldreher executed a quarterback sneak from the Tech 1 for the 13-3 final score.

Paul Castner turned in a performance for the ages when ND met Indiana for the Irish homecoming. In the 27-0 Notre Dame victory, Castner scored all the points: he drop-kicked field goals of 45 and 35 yards, scored TDs on the ground from the Hoosier 20 and 22, intercepted a Hoosier pass from their 35 and took it in for another TD, and booted three PATs. Maybe his teammates thought he could do it all, but he couldn't and Notre Dame next tied Army 0-0. Both teams seemed tight; it was a game of lost opportunities. Both teams drove deep into the other's red zone but failed to score. Castner fumbled at the Cadet 4, then tried to atone for his miscue with a 55-yard field goal ... but he was operating with a sprained ankle and a broken nose and the kick fell short.

Rockne did what he could to see his big fullback nursed into playing shape for the game against Butler.

But Fate dealt Paul Castner a cruel blow early in the Butler game when he went down hard in a pileup. At first, it was thought that it was a dislocated hip, but it was actually broken. Butler lost the game 31-3, and Rockne's fertile football mind went into overtime to work out a way of replacing his All-American fullback.

In the Rockne system, the "star" position, the dominant player, was the left halfback position. To this point in the season, Elmer Layden had played this crucial position. Rockne asked him to move to the fullback spot, replacing the lost Castner, and Jim Crowley moved up from the second team to take over the left halfback spot. Stuhldreher by this point was getting most of the starting time at QB. And, just like that, Rockne had his dream backfield. … at least in its football infancy. What he now had was a splendid blending of four players with a keen knack for timing, speed, power, rhythm, and the guile needed for operating this sophisticated offense.

These four players just had something about them that would make their use of the shift as devastating as any offense could be. Today's readers need to keep in mind the difficulty in executing this tactic: the backfield might line up in a straight T formation, but shift into the Notre Dame box:

To do this, the backs each had to move different distances in the same amount of time, using the same

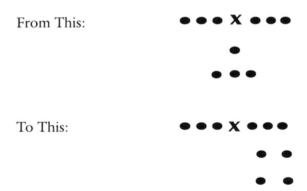

number of steps. For instance, the quarterback might not have far to move, but the right halfback would have to move up slightly and over diagonally two yards, the left halfback would have to move parallel to the line of scrimmage six and a half feet, and the fullback only four feet or so. Occasionally, an end would also move, in or out, depending on the set. Rockne had his backfields practice this intricate maneuver in slow motion until they had the timing down perfectly. As mentioned earlier, when the whole thing worked as designed, it virtually overwhelmed a defense at the point of attack.

Their first try together was against a good Carnegie Tech team. Ironically, Carnegie Tech opened up the game with 1905 vintage mass plays, good for two quick first downs. The Irish defense recovered and started to take charge. 1905 football then met modern Notre Dame football and the Irish took it to the Scots for a 19-0 win—their sixth shutout of the season. Nebraska proved to be a different story, playing consistent football for a 14-6 win, ending the Irish season in a game played before Gen. Pershing as an honored guest. Nebraska racked up two TDs in the second quarter; the only Irish response was a TD pass from Layden to Miller. The rest of the offense was stymied by a powerful Nebraska defense.

The 1922 season had been a transitional one, although it hadn't really started out that way. The seniors had played with Gipp; when Castner went down, there was a glimmer of the future Four Horsemen as Rockne re-arranged the backfield. Surely he knew he had a pretty good thing going here ... it's doubtful, however, that he knew fully just how good this group would become.

In 1923, when Rockne started his sixth season under the Dome, he had already stayed at Notre Dame longer than any previous Irish head coach. With a 39-3-3 record, for a winning percentage of .922, he was behind only Jack Marks, whose two-year stint of 13-0-2 produced a .933 winning percentage. Jesse Harper was the only other Irish head coach at that point in Notre Dame's football history with five years served as head coach. His

Rockne in his anti-superstition #13 coaching garb.

record through the 1917 season stood at 34-5-1, an .863 winning percentage. Among those who followed Rockne, Frank Leahy's first five seasons resulted in a 39-7-4 record, a winning percentage of .820. Ara Parseghian's record stood at 41-7-3, for a winning percentage of .833. Dan Devine's teams went 44-14-0 in his first five seasons, good for a .758 winning percentage. Lou Holtz's record came to 46-14-0, a winning percentage of .766. When we consider that one-third of Rockne's losses and two-thirds of his teams' ties through 1922 happened in the relatively disastrous 1918 season, when everything that could go wrong did go wrong, and then some, we can better sense the nature of Rockne's dominance and the full nature of his achievement. Furthermore, we can empathize with the challenge that rings down through the echoes of history to every coach who ever followed Rockne under the Dome. These are all extremely competent, highly competitive, deeply dedicated men. They know their craft well, certainly better than most. They have to play tough opposition and, no matter the outcome, they are measured against Rockne's incredible attainments. And today's coaches don't have Kalamazoo to beat up on anymore.

Speaking of Kalamazoo, they were the opening competition in 1923 and they were steamrolled 74-0.

Rockne started his shock troops. Sub Red Maher shocked Kalamazoo, all right—he took the opening kickoff and zipped 90 yards for a TD...but give credit to his teammates, who flattened all eleven opposing players. On Maher's next carry, he scooted 53 yards; next, he scored from 7 yards out. Miller scored from 59 yards out...Crowley bettered that, scoring from 68 yards away. Rockne shared the TD spoils among a bevy of players. Kalamazoo never earned a first down, though they often had very good seats from which to watch the Irish TD parade. It was the last time ND would schedule them in football.

Army scouted the next game, Lombard, and the Irish won by the slim margin of 14-0. Rockne purposely did not give the Army scouts much to see. His play book for a season was slim in the first place, so limiting the team to a conservative game plan meant that Army went back home with nothing much.

It didn't get any better for Army when they ran into the Irish on the field at Ebbets Field in New York (an early measure of how big this game was becoming). Before a capacity crowd of 30,000, Army fielded a very large, physical team. Rockne's Irish were lean and quick. The final score was 13-0 for the Irish, but ND dominated far more than that score reveals—compiling 13 first downs to Army's 2, snagging 3 interceptions in the 11 passes the Cadets tried, 3 more than Army caught (apparently, they had not improved much in the passing game since Rockne helped beat them ten years earlier), 49 yards rushing to ND's 165.

The next eastern victim was one of the original Big Three—Princeton. They were undefeated since 1921, but Notre Dame spanked them 25-2 and overwhelmed them pretty much as they had Army: 27 first downs to 5, 465 yards of total offense to 101, 241 yards rushing to 54. All four of the young Horsemen were involved in scoring or setting up a score.

Purdue was the Homecoming opponent once again. Don Miller played well—with four runs over 25

The Irish in action against eastern powerhouse Princeton.

yards each, two TDs, and 50 yards in receptions. The final score was 34-7.

Pep rally for ND students circa 1923.

With eastern football more or less flattened and in the rear view mirror, the Irish hosted a team from the south, Georgia Tech, and handled them with ease, 35-7. Miller had TD runs of 59 and 23 yards and lost an 88-yard score on a penalty. Red Maher spelled Miller at one point. Tech thought they might relax, but if they did, Maher made them pay with a 46-yard TD run. Tackle Joe Bach blocked two Tech punts, one going to end Gene Mayl for a TD. Purdue was the Homecoming opponent once again. Don Miller played well—with four runs over 25 yards each, two TDs, and 50 yards in receptions. The final score was 34-7.

One more time, Nebraska spoiled the 1923 party with a 14-7 win. They choked off the Irish offense with a great pass defense. Rockne countered by running in some enthusiastic subs in the third quarter. Bill Cerney snagged a 20-yard TD pass from Stuhldreher, but that was all the Irish could muster. Twice in a row the Huskers had placed a blot on the scutcheon of Notre Dame's seasons. Rockne must have been having nightmares about Nebraska. In his one novel about football, *The Four Winners*, published in 1925 (maybe writing was therapeutic

Rockne coaching in more formal attire.

for him), he made the evil opposition for his fictional team be called "Aksarben"—Nebraska spelled backwards.

The 1924 Notre Dame football season has to be considered among the finest anywhere, any time. Rockne proved to be the master of all that he could do on the national stage of football drama. The line was determined, powerful, and very quick; the backfield as a unit was probably the best Rockne had mustered They were speedy, elusive, smart, and consummate competitors.

Lombard replaced Kalamazoo (outscored 284-0 in their six games with the Irish) for the opener, but fared only marginally better in a 40-0 Notre Dame win even though Stuhldreher sat out the game. Miller scored twice, subs ran 50 and 57 yards for scores, and Crowley and Cerney tallied. Similarly, Wabash played its final game versus Notre Dame and went down 34-0. Rockne played subs most of the way, for the non-benefit of Army scouts. Crowley scored on one of his classic, long end runs and Ward Connell scored on another long run, dragging five hapless Wabash defenders into the endzone with him.

The 1924 game with Army completed the process of Notre Dame's transition from a state football power to a regional phenomenon to a national force. Rockne had come to be seen as the virtual personification of all that was good in college football. Based on their exploits in this memorable game, his superb little backfield would be immortalized as media heroes in ways unknown before Grantland Rice wrote his famous story of this game. For the rest of his career, Rockne and his teams would play at a level of excellence virtually unattainable by other coaches and teams.

Both teams were undefeated going into the game—and loaded with talent. The SRO Polo Grounds crowd reached 55,000...almost twice the number of spectators at any previous ND game and nearly as large as the total number of fans to see the marvelous George Gipp in all Notre Dame games in 1919, just five years before. The game was played carefully between evenly matched personnel. The first quarter was used mainly for probing into strengths and weaknesses...the punting game dominated. The Irish took the initiative in the second quarter, starting from their own 15-yard line. In seven well-designed plays, the Irish slashed through the Cadets, using six

The starting eleven for the undefeated 1924 Irish, Seven Mules and Four Horsemen.

runs and one pass, Layden earning the scoring honors. Layden also got ND going in the third quarter with an interception; Crowley wrapped up the opportunity when he ran a flanking pattern past a flailing West Point end for a 20-yard TD. The Cadets came right back, with one 45-yard run shocking the Irish into alertness. Eventually, substandard Irish punts allowed Army to score, leaving the final score 13-7 for a Notre Dame win. Even though it was a low-scoring game, its ebb and flow, stunning plays, and courageous personal exploits made a tremendous impact on the spectators.

Rockne's pal, sportswriter Grantland Rice.

Grantland Rice, a close friend of Rockne's, had been standing on the sidelines in the 1923 ND-Army game at Ebbets Field when he was almost pulverized by Irish backs running loose around end, slammed out of bounds by Army's fierce defenders. He had remarked to a friend then that it was like being run over by a stampede of horses. Perhaps the memory and the remark lingered in the back of Rice's mind. During the 1924 game, he was seated in the press box near Rockne's student press aide, George Strickler, safely out of range of Rockne's backfield. Strickler had recently seen Rudolph Valentino's 1921 movie, "The Four Horsemen of the Apocalypse," and observed to those around him in the press box that the Irish backfield's stunning deeds recalled images from the Valentino film. Throughout the game, Grantland Rice found himself amazed by the grace and power of the Notre Dame backfield, and echoes of the 1923 incident ran through his mind. Perhaps Strickler's comment stuck there too. In any case, Rice wrote an inspired story on the game for the October 19 issue of the *New York Herald Tribune*. It has become the most famous example of sports writing in American journalism:

> *Outlined against a blue, gray October sky*
> *the Four Horsemen rode again. In dramatic*
> *lore they are known as famine, pestilence,*
> *destruction and death. These are only*
> *aliases. Their real names are Stuhldreher,*
> *Miller, Crowley and Layden ...*

These few sentences in a New York daily took Rockne, his backfield, and Notre Dame to a different plane of public awareness. George Strickler, by the way, wasn't finished contributing in this matter. Shortly after the team's return to Notre Dame, he rounded up four horses and posed the Irish backfield on them for a publicity photo—which has taken on a life of it own, like Rice's prose. (Note that Crowley is not exactly sitting comfortably in the photo—he had a small problem with his backside and had to lean slightly to one side). Later, Strickler became the sports editor of the *Chicago Tribune*. The Horsemen didn't do too badly later in life either. But before their fame earned as young men helped launch them in their careers, along with Rockne and their teammates, they

The Horsemen later in life,
four very successful men.

Horseman and right halfback Don Miller poses near the stands of old Cartier Field.

had to run the gauntlet of large crowds, a parade, and endless speeches upon their return to South Bend.

We know what Rockne thought of distractions (one wonders what he thought of the time spent with the Horsemen posing for Strickler's photo). So, while he must have enjoyed the adulation the team was receiving, he had to get them ready for Princeton, one of the vestigial pieces of evidence from the former days of Eastern college football dominance. Rockne was fully aware of this (remember, little more than a decade before this illustrious season, the eastern press had Notre Dame coming from Illinois). He had some plans for Princeton.

Part of the plan was to showcase his left halfback, Crowley. This part of the plan worked very well...Crowley broke loose for 250 almost uncontested yards rushing and the two TDs in the 12-0 ND win. Along the way, the Irish squelched Princeton's offense, holding them to four first downs (while accumulating 20 of their own). The Irish shock troops played halfway into the second quarter and had things well in hand when they turned the game over to the first team...the Tigers had gained a total of 1.5 yards in 20 rushing attempts. But the *piece de resistance* in Rockne's plan was reserved for the second half Princeton kickoff—he had the Irish return the ball in a flying wedge formation, surely the death knell for the kind of football represented by that troglodytic formation, a brand of football that Rockne's version would replace all over the country. Two unusual plays, however, could not have been rehearsed: Crowley's second TD saw him bounce off no less than four putative Princeton tacklers...and Miller managed to get spun around and make a 35-yard advance while running backwards. With that, it all seems to have worked for Rockne against Princeton that day.

Notre Dame football had started in 1887, with a single late November game in the season, a loss to Michigan. Four months later, Rockne was born in Voss, Norway. The surviving members of that 1887 team were invited to be the guests of honor for the 1924 Homecoming Game, against Georgia Tech, thus uniting crucial elements of the developing history of Notre Dame football. The Irish won it—appropriately ND's 200th victory—by a 34-3 margin. Stuhldreher was not able to play; Red Edwards spelled him, but Georgia Tech couldn't stop his orchestrating the Irish offense anyway. In a way, the microdetails of the game are not too important...the Four Horsemen, were fully involved in all the scoring drives (it must have been a nightmare defensing their slashing methods of offense), but as impressive is the fact that their substitutes worked the same magic, scoring on virtually identical plays as had the starters. It was Rockne's system at its best, a clear indication that he had succeeded in blending the personnel with the offense designed to maximize their particular gifts.

Wisconsin managed a 3-3 tie...against the shock troops. Then the starters came in and slammed the door on that, scoring four touchdowns before returning the game back to the subs. Crowley scored twice, once with a Stuhldreher pass, and Miller and Layden tacked on a score each. John Roach scored after Joe Harmon pulled in an errant Wisconsin pass, making it a 38-3 final.

Nebraska. Aksarben. Always the Huskers, always tough, always a threat to ruin an otherwise great Notre Dame season. Well, that's how it seems, but it had only happened in 1922 and 1923. Rockne wanted this one terribly, as did the players. But it started out disastrously when the Huskers fell on an Irish fumble and scored as a result. This must have energized the Irish, because they roared back for a 34-6 win. In the second quarter, Stuhldreher and Miller scored in fairly quick succession, then Miller did it again in the third quarter. Crowley hauled in a pass and rambled 65 yards with a pass Stuhldreher had thrown from the prone position (legal in those days). The Irish kept it basic and slammed the middle insistently, Layden scoring the final TD. The statistics showed the Irish domination that day: 465 yards rushing to 56, 24 first downs to 3, 8 of 11 passes completed for 101 yards to 1 of 7 for 20 yards. It was a total team effort and must have done much to have assuaged the bitter feelings from the prior two losses.

Northwestern was a very different story. Against the subs, they managed to stay in ND's end of the field, garnering two field goals in the process. Rockne had seen enough … the starters came in and tuned up the passing game. Stuhldreher fired a pass to Crowley who turned it into a long gainer to the Wildcat 9 yard line. A quarter-back sneak for a TD two plays later capped the drive. Two plays later, Stuhldreher intercepted a Northwestern pass and hauled it 40 yards for the winning TD in a 13-6 thriller. Carnegie Tech, a team that would play the Irish tough for more than a decade, closed out the regular season with a loss to Notre Dame, 40-19, their three scores being the most TDs scored on the Irish since Army's 30-10 win over ND in 1916. The Scots had the game tied 13-13 at the half. Notre Dame's passing game, however, proved to be the difference. At one point, Rockne's offense completed 12 passes in a row. Half of Notre Dame's six TDs came through the air. Captain and center Adam Walsh, living evidence of how tough the game was contested, was knocked out six times in the course of the game before being taken off the field.

Notre Dame's undefeated season had once again aroused the attention of the Rose Bowl Committee. After some start and stop negotiations, ND settled to play Pop Warner's Stanford team (having rejected Haskell and being originally rejected by Stanford). Rockne did not miss the chance to showcase the Irish at numerous stops during the marathon train journey to and from the West coast. In spite of the adulation and banquets, the team reached the coast about eight pounds lighter, on average, per man.

On paper, the Irish looked like they could use the extra weight against Warner's team, led as it was by All-American fullback Ernie Nevers. Warner's single-wing offense was designed to control the clock, sustain long drives with incremental gains, and generally pound on the defense. It was the 1920's version of the "three yards

The complete 1924 team.

and a cloud of dust" approach to the game. Stanford would, however, put the ball in the air, as scouting reports to Rockne revealed. And these passes, Rockne learned, would be tipped off by the fact that Nevers would swing out a little wider on his route out of the backfield. Rockne took the cue on this and coached his defensive backs to change their alignment ever so slightly in order to have a good angle on the ensuing pass. His players later said that Rockne "coached in inches"—and this game was a perfect example of such attention to detail. The plan worked...Stanford, not surprisingly, "won" the statistics but lost the game, 27-10. An alert Irish defense intercepted five Stanford passes, with Layden reacting perfectly to the tip-off by Nevers, spearing two Stanford passes and returning them for TDs on runbacks of 78 and 70 yards. Another ND score followed a fumbled punt, Ed Hunsinger the lucky opportunist to chug 20 yards to the end zone. Warner's offense was designed to gain ground—and did; Rockne's offense was designed to score from anywhere, anytime—and did. (Warner once proposed that first downs be awarded one point toward the final score, an idea whose time never came). Rockne's approach to football—and this impressive win—guaranteed

Ernie Nevers.

that football would be a game of initiative and opportunity, not mere territorial control and clock management. Warner's approach was not unrelated to the ponderous game that Rockne's coaching left behind.

After the big win, the weary players wandered up and down and around on a meandering train ride back to the campus. Rockne and the team garnered more good will (and probably some ill will as well...what else is new

for the Irish?) with numerous stops and festivities. When they got back to the Dome, four of them had been named All-Americans—Layden, Stuhldreher, Crowley, and Walsh. For his part, Rockne had led the Irish in seven football campaigns, with three of them posting undefeated seasons, the other four with one loss each...a .915 winning percentage, based on a stunning 58-4-3 record. With all this going for him, it's not a big surprise that Rockne would be in increasing public demand.

As a result of the adulation and attention he was receiving, Rockne responded with two publications—*Coaching* and *The Four Winners*. Coaching is exactly what it says, a series of questions and answers regarding various game situations, obviously modeled on the "classes" in football that he sponsored at Notre Dame. It contains many sound coaching principles. Adjusting for rules changes, much of the coaching wisdom here is still pertinent today.

1924 Captain Adam Walsh, a comedian of the era, and Rockne, who must be wondering if all the fame is really worth it at times like this.

The Four Winners duplicates some of the coaching business material from the former publication. Yet this is a novel, to be sure, no threat to Nobel laureates, but the essential Rockne comes through nicely. Brains, deception, and speed are always preferred over brawn, mass play, and slow, sheer bulk. His QB, Elmer Higgins, is a youngster with brains who overcomes physical limitations to become a team leader. Other characters in the novel represent some of Rockne's pet peeves—the lounge lizard, the backslider, the blowhard coach. The novel also expresses Rockne's sincere belief of the social role of football and the importance of campus "spirit" for a fully meaningful college career. There are parades and pep rallies celebrating each game; anxious word of injuries to key players spreads quickly around the campus. Rockne portrays a university in which the life of the institution seems to revolve primarily around the unfolding melodrama of the football season. Perhaps this is really what Rockne believed should be the case. Rhetorically, however, he argued for a balance between the life of the mind and the physical expression of the body in athletics. Still, he seems a bit torn over this classic dualism. He was a very smart man, yes, but he had obviously cast his lot with the playing of football and the profession of coaching football. Indeed, the conflict is one that has haunted both the general world of higher education, but Notre Dame specifically. And Knute Rockne is central to this. Perhaps it is both unwise and unfair to expect such a seminal figure in

Knute and Bonnie Rockne, with Illinois head coach Bob Zuppke—
yet another Renaissance college football coach of this age.
(Below) Rockne and a movie starlet of the day.

the institution of collegiate football to be free of such conflicts.

Rockne may have been a bit of a compulsive personality. Not only did he throw himself into writing, but he seems to have been unable to say no to other ventures and demands. He launched into public speaking, became a tour guide to the 1928 Amsterdam Olympics, a stock broker, screenplay consultant, playwright consultant, an entrepreneur for a variety of football clinics, and a motivational speaker for the Studebaker Corporation. By 1925, he was not serving anymore as Notre Dame's track coach and his involvement in teaching chemistry was a thing of the past. He may have been one of the early examples of how popular fame and success can pull a personality in multiple directions. It does seem that Rockne thrived under such pressure, even though he was working at a pace that would have killed a lesser man.

With the 1925 season, Rockne had invested fifteen years of his life in Notre Dame. For all of that time, he well remembered being one of the few Protestants at Irish Catholic Notre Dame. He had respected the Catholicism of the large majority of his players; he also encouraged his Protestant brethren to be team leaders. But even in their team prayers, they reverted to the use of Catholic prayers in team meetings, pregame preparations and the like. The lived religious reality on the Notre Dame campus is challenging, receptive, ubiquitous and thorough. Over the years of his career, Rockne had thus been heavily exposed to the values and practices of Roman Catholicism. It is to be expected, then, that Rockne would be a good candidate for an eventual conversion. He began to study the Catholic catechism under the instruction of Father Vincent Mooney, a process that took several months of intensive study. On November 20, 1925, Rockne received the Catholic sacrament of Baptism. On the following day, in the Log Chapel on the Notre Dame campus, Rockne received his first Holy Communion as a Catholic. Later that day, he led the team against Northwestern—and used the occasion of his conversion to goad his players at the halftime of a game they were losing. Oddly enough, he also manged to have one of his well-documented contract flings even as he was in the process of converting and working through the Irish football season.

Even as Rockne's public career took off (beyond his summer football camps and the like), the 1925 season loomed with major challenges. Not the least of these was that the entire starting eleven from 1924 had graduated. Rockne had never been faced with replacing his entire starting team. (This would be the equivalent in today's college football of having to replace both the starting offensive and the defensive units). Of course, his shock troop system gave him a good pool from which to draw. Tackle Joe Boland, fullback Rex Enright, and a promising sophomore halfback named Christie Flanagan headlined a blue collar group of players who had the job of taking over for the departed 1924 National Champs.

Their task did not appear any easier by virtue of the fact that the opening opponent was Baylor, two-time defending Southwest Conference champs. Unfortunately for Baylor, they must have forgotten how to complete a forward pass ... Notre Dame won the game 41-0 while Baylor failed to complete a single pass in 15 attempts (as opposed to ND's 8 for 11 passing). Rockne used eight different running backs in the game and spread around the scoring. After that, Lombard was the next team to fall to the Irish, by a 69-0 mark. Dick Hanousek tallied three of ND's 10 TDs. In between the thrill of these touchdowns, fans must have wondered what the heck the Irish were doing, standing around after a play in a tight circle. In fact, Rockne had them operating out of a huddle, as opposed to the then-prevailing practice of getting up and going directly to the line of scrimmage for the next play (which was called out from a sequence of numbers by the Irish quarterback). With this win, the Irish had 15 in a row, half of them shutouts.

Beloit took care of the shutout possibility by going up 3-0 on a surprised Notre Dame team. They weren't

Tackle Joe Boland—later the longtime voice of the Irish on radio.

finished with surprises either, since they also pulled off the first screen pass the Irish had seen. Harry O'Boyle got the initial score for the Irish, and Joe Prelli launched himself on a 67-yard TD jaunt for a solid lead. Lew Cody intercepted a Beloit pass then bolted 47 yards for the final score of a 19-3 win.

Army had only one tie to show for the previous seven contests with Notre Dame, but they got a measure of revenge for all those disappointments with a convincing 27-0 win. They had Rockne's team well-scouted and the personnel to dominate the game.

For years Notre Dame had been trying to gain admittance to the Big 10. This had never come to pass but the Irish kept looking for Big 10 opponents. The 1925 season saw ND travel to Minnesota for its first game with that school. Well into the third quarter, Rockne had to watch a lackluster performance, the game tied 7-7. But the Gophers made the first big mistake with a terrible punt that led to a 28-yard drive capped by a Flanagan TD. A Minnesota fumble on the next series sealed their fate, Enright scoring from the 4-yard line two plays later, making it a 19-7 final score. The Gophers kept shooting themselves in the paw, fumbling at the Irish 2, Art Parisien going 80 yards with the recovered ball.

Rockne's teams were steadily earning a reputation for their peregrinations. Some pundits called the team "Rockne's Ramblers." After the trip to Minnesota, they moved on to old foe Georgia Tech. An interception (notice how often Rockne's teams played outstanding defense) started the Irish momentum. Flanagan scored to end a 25-yard drive; in the second quarter, he exploded on two long runs before tacking on his second TD. Another interception doomed a Tech drive and secured the 13-0 ND victory.

Knute Rockne.

From the deep south, Rockne took his team to the east to play Penn State. Miserable weather had made the field nearly unplayable. The Irish overcame the mud to run well enough until they reached the red zone, then Penn State shut them down. Enright tried a 13-yard field goal but he missed it. The teams slipped and slid into a 0-0 tie.

For the Homecoming Game, the Irish whipped Carnegie Tech 26-0. Rockne used shock troops for the better part of two quarters, then the starters probed for two possessions before striking pay dirt. Enright was prominent on the first scoring drive, but Flanagan tallied the score. Enright scored twice in the third quarter, the second coming on a fumble recovery. The subs wrapped up the scoring.

Northwestern came to the Golden Dome and staked out a halftime lead of 10-0. This turn of events had not taken place for a long, long time. Rockne had to do something to awaken his players and he gave them a piece of his mind at the half about this insulting situation, wondering aloud about the efficacy of his conversion to Catholicism. In consecutive possessions, Enright and Flanagan sparked drives and scored, allowing the Irish to reclaim a 13-10 lead for the win.

The season finale was with Nebraska, but Rockne would have to do it without Flanagan, who was injured. Nebraska was coming off a free weekend and was free of injuries. Rockne followed the usual script and started the shock troops, but Nebraska manhandled them, racking up two TDs in the first quarter (arcane, rigid substitution rules did not allow for a quick recovery in such situations … today's rules would have facilitated a faster remedy to such a situation). Notre Dame's passing game failed utterly—the Irish completed one miserable pass in twelve tries. The Huskers tacked on a third-quarter field goal and copped a 17-0 win.

Almost any coach can have a great season with superb athletic material. Wind 'em up and turn 'em loose. Rockne had more or less been able to do precisely that in 1919, 1920, and 1924. Coaches have to show their mettle when they are not overstocked with the best talent. This is what Rockne faced in 1925. It's a rare day in Notre Dame football history when an entire starting unit has to be replaced, but that's what Rockne had to do. To call it a rebuilding year would be an understatement. He had to identify and mentor the team leaders. He really had to teach some football to relatively inexperienced personnel. He had to match his tactics to the personnel, and probably take a few calculated risks that he might not otherwise chance. He had to find the right balance in coaching methods for his bright sophomores, letting them get their feet wet without running the risk of drowning them. His 7-2-1 record, an exact match for Parseghian's 1965 record, would likewise prove to be a transitional season sandwiched between two superlative campaigns.

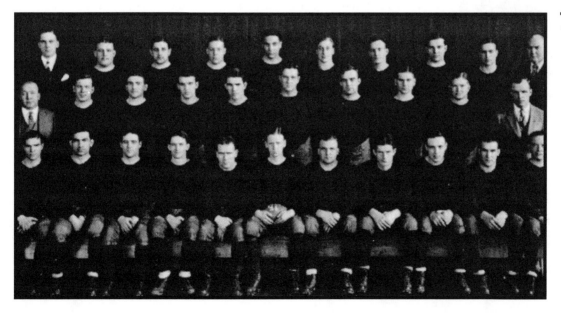

The 1926 Fighting Irish won nine for Rockne.

When the 1926 season started, the anti-shift forces had managed to lobby well enough that a full-second stop after a backfield shift was mandated. In 1924, the Four Horsemen could shift just before the snap, allowing their momentum to be a factor in the ensuing play and also creating chaos for the defense, with the sudden change in alignment. The rules change for the 1926 season was the beginning of a drawn-out process that would eventually see the shift as Rockne evolved it become a thing of football's past. Rockne claimed that the objection to the shift was not really with the tactic itself, but with himself and the Irish as a team. In short, it was a case of envy.

Along with this change, the Irish would be playing the first coast-to-coast season schedule ever for a college team (the pro game was still pretty much an eastern and midwestern phenomenon). The grand tour at the end of the 1924 season, to and from the Rose Bowl, showed Rockne that it was possible to do the planning, practicing, and logistics without seriously hampering the team's effectiveness in a game. (One wonders about the academic ramifications). The negotiations leading to the game itself included a tempting offer from USC, a connection Rockne would maximize in short order, in time to fold USC into the 1926 season.

Rockne had one breather to start the season, Beloit, and the Irish dispatched them in short order 77-0. Eleven ND players scored, with Flanagan's 95-yard kickoff return being the best of the lot. Vince McNally racked up two more; the others tallied one TD each, including one by future star, Jack Chevigny. Minnesota was a different story, but two long TD runs, 65 yards each, by Bucky Dahman and Christie Flanagan, and a 15-yard TD burst by Tom Hearden near the end of the game held Minnesota at bay for a 20-7 Irish win. The downside—tackle Joe Boland and fullback Fred Collins were lost for the season with injuries.

Penn State had been brooding over the 0-0 tie from 1925; coach Hugo Bedzek had worked his players hard. But the Irish had the fast track they lacked in the 1925 game. QB Art Parisien and Harry O'Boyle teamed up for a catch and run play that covered 50 yards for ND's first TD. Penn State could not sustain a drive, punted, and Parisien and O'Boyle struck again, from 53 yards out. Penn State held the Irish offense in check for

Fred Collins, starting fullback
on the 1928 team.

four straight possessions, but Red Edwards broke it open with a 45-yards TD scamper. Jack Chevigny ended the scoring by breaking seven tackles on the way to a 17-yard TD run. Notre Dame won handily 28-0, gaining 506 yards to Penn State's 85 yards.

Northwestern used its home date to dedicate its new stadium. Pumped up, they nearly whipped the Irish, but eventually succumbed 6-0. With about 5 minutes to go in the game, Rockne sent in Parisien, who promptly fired a pass good for 66 yards to Chile Walsh, then a 14-yard TD strike to Chevigny. The Irish used good punts to hold Northwestern in check; Tom Hearden snagged a Wildcat pass to seal the win. The Irish next faced Georgia Tech, copping a 12-0 win by virtue of John Roach's short yardage TD run, and good passing by Niemiec to set the stage for another short TD run, this by Bucky Dahman.

Rockne's defense was sparkling: beating Indiana next 26-0 meant five out of the last six Irish games produced goose eggs for the opposition. Flanagan scored on a short TD burst and then again on a long, zig-zag sideline-to-sideline run. Bucky Dahman tacked on two more second-half scores for the final total.

The great defense would be needed against a solid Army team, a team that had whipped the Irish pretty bad in '25. Coming home on the train from that game, Rockne did a "pre-year" exhortation, asking the players to dedicate themselves to the task of beating Army in '26. This they did, 7-0, in one of those games that ought to be preserved in amber. The game's only score came on one of Rockne's favorites, the "51" play—left halfback Flanagan off tackle for a 68-yard TD … the quintessential perfect play.

The shutouts kept coming as Drake expired 21-0. Drake did manage to play evenly with the scrubs, at one point even reaching the Irish 3-inch line. The defense held and turned over the game to the starters, who drove 95 yards for a score, Edwards earning the honor with a 2-yard QB sneak. Drake started a drive in response, but John Wallace hauled in an interception and rumbled 30 yards for a TD. O'Boyle caught a TD pass in a snowfall to complete the scoring.

Rockne's team was riding high. For the weekend of the Carnegie Tech game, the coach had plans to go to Chicago, attend the Army-Navy game, and meet Pop Warner and Tad Jones to make All-American selections. He entrusted the team to Hunk Anderson. Pride goeth before a fall. The Tech coach, Walter Steffen, milked Rockne's absence for all he could in pre-game remarks to his team. The Techsters came out fired up, the Irish obviously did not regard them very highly, and Anderson turned out not to be a Rockne as a coach (as would be clearly demonstrated again in the 1931-33 seasons). When the smoke settled, Rockne must have nearly choked on his cigar to learn that Notre Dame had lost its undefeated season, ironically in a 19-0 shutout, to an inspired Carnegie Tech team.

To complete the season and the coast-to-coast schedule, ND had its first encounter with USC, starting up one of the most stirring intersectional rivalries in collegiate athletics. To start the series and the game, ND scored first, with QB Charles Riley faking a plunge into the line only to break the play outside for a 20-yard TD run. The Trojans countered this with a TD following an interception; both teams missed the extra-point attempts. The game settled into a stalemate until the fourth quarter, when USC's Wheeler strung together five runs covering 44 yards and a TD. The Trojans missed this conversion kick as well, making it 12-6. The Irish floundered around helplessly; Rockne had to do something. With but 90 seconds remaining in the game, Rockne sent in his diminutive QB, Art Parisien. He knew what to do—fire passes, and Niemiec grabbed a pair, covering 50 yards, including the second TD of the day for the Irish. The kick was good and ND left La-La-land with a 13-12 victory. No one

Art Boeringer, starting center for the '26 Irish.

then could have known it for sure, but the thrilling conclusion to the game would be replicated often enough in the decades ahead between these two great football programs. For their good work in a great but marred season, center Art Boeringer was a first-team All-American and Christie Flanagan earned second-team honors.

The long train ride back from LA gave Rockne plenty of time to mull over the Carnegie Tech fiasco. Perhaps it crossed his mind that he was becoming over-committed in his personal dealings outside the Notre Dame football scene. He and Bonnie had children to consider, however, and there were opportunities ga-lore for him to choose among in order to strengthen the family's security. His face was rapidly becoming one of the better known icons in America. He was alive in the heyday of the supposed Golden Age of American sports. The Depression had yet to set in, forever alter-ing an entire generation's sense of what could be done in a life. Perhaps, as with many Americans, all things seemed truly possible; unlimited progress seemed to be the order of the day. Twenty-twenty hindsight is acutely perceptive; today we can see the gathering problems and complexities. Rockne had big plans emerging in his mind, including a major construction project for a new stadium to replace worn-out Cartier Field. He knew he was a commodity. He would have to choose wisely, judiciously from among the many options before him—writing, business, travel, other coaching positions; he would be unable not to choose.

One thing was for sure—Rockne had invested enough of his life in the game of football at this point that the deep attachment to it, from the depths of his being, was occasionally seen by others in ways that the coach seldom allowed. One instance in particular, detailed in Tim Cohane's book, *Great College Football Coaches of the Twenties and Thirties,* involved Allan Messick, who had been an assistant coach during Rockne's playing days. He was with Rockne the night before the Irish were to start their long train ride to the west coast to play USC. He and Rockne took a walk around the Notre Dame campus, ending up at Cartier Field. Rockne took Messick to a place just in front of one of the goalposts. Messick saw that Rockne was becoming emotional, deeply moved by the flood of associations and memories. In front of the goalposts, Rockne stood in silence with his eyes closed. Then he knelt and kissed the ground. Schmaltzy, yes; sincere, yes. The incident reveals the depths of Rockne's deep spiritual attachment to this game that had done so much to form the man.

The starting eleven for the 1927 Irish.

As much as the man loved the place and the game, there was always work to be done to stay on top of the collegiate game. The 1927 edition of the Irish had a good returning core from the '26 campaign, with Flanagan heading the list. The left side of the line returned intact, but Rockne would have to rebuild the right side of the line and fill the three remaining backfield spots to accompany Flanagan. The schedule was not quite as demanding as in 1926; the Irish would stay on the eastern side of the Mississippi for almost all of their games, although Navy was added to the list, a game to be played in Baltimore. With the addition of the Midshipmen, Rockne initiated yet another intersectional series that would persist for three quarters of a century (and possibly well beyond). He also thereby helped establish an institutional relationship that flourished over the years, one that was especially crucial in the World War II years for the U. S. Navy chose Notre Dame as one of its sites for training officer candidates. The infusion of these students came during some very lean years for Notre Dame, as many in its all-male student body were away meeting their patriotic duties in the armed services. Former University President Rev. Theodore Hesburgh (who was the chaplain to ND's returning vets after the war) has often claimed that this decision saved the university, which in turn feels obligated to continue the football series with

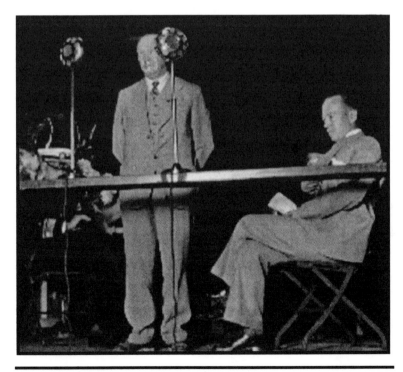

Rockne giving a pre-game talk.

Navy, even when the talent pool is often one-sided. Perhaps the U. S. Navy would have reached this decision independent of a football series, but many of the top-line officers in the war years had either played in or enjoyed watching these contests, and obviously Notre Dame came to mind for them as a good site for one of their war years programs. As with many spin-off effects of the Rockne years, the resonances have continued to echo through the years and decades since his time. The balding student who showed up at Notre Dame in 1910 will likely have an ongoing impact on many facets of the University of Notre Dame well into a new century.

Navy was scheduled for the third game of the '27 season. As usual, Rockne kept things fairly simple for the early games, before a major opponent. Coe went down 28-7 and Detroit lost 20-7 ... but careful observers might have noted that this was not an Irish team that could score at will as some had under Rockne, especially against weaker opponents. It was also fairly obvious that the team was not stocked with depth at all positions; after certain starters, there was quite a gap.

Rockne took the team to Baltimore, on the usual train ride, for the opening game of the Navy series. Niemiec put the Irish in an early hole when he bobbled a punt at the ND 6. Navy scored in short order; Rockne sensed the threat was real and pulled the subs. The game stayed at 6-0 for Navy until the third quarter ... then the Irish defense blocked two punts, the second resulting in a TD for Chile Walsh. On the next Irish possession, Rockne turned loose Flanagan—for a 35-yard gain off tackle, then 25 yards around right end. Charlie Riley then zipped around the left end for a 12-yard TD scamper. Niemiec got back the TD he caused earlier for Navy with good passing near the end of the game, capped with his own TD to make the final score 19-6.

The Irish next visited in-state rival Indiana. The Hoosiers scored first when a back outran the subs early in the game for a 45-yard TD burst. Niemiec got that back in the second quarter with a 1-yard TD plunge. In the third quarter, Dahman put the Irish in the lead to cap a five-play drive with a TD burst, then Flanagan racked up the final TD for the same score as against Navy, 19-6. The Irish had not shown an ability to run a high-scoring offense; their defense was keeping them in these games.

Georgia Tech, undefeated, came north but ran into a determined Notre Dame team. They still did not turn in a dominating performance, but Tech never really had any part of the game in hand. The subs did

Starting right halfback for the 1927 team, Bucky Dahman.

well enough this time, turning over a 0-0 game after one quarter to the starters, who began to move the ball immediately. Fullback Fred Collins set up his own TD with a 20-yard scamper, then pushed it in with a 17-yard TD run to open the scoring. Tech obligingly fumbled and Collins scored again, from the Tech 25 yard line. In the fourth quarter, Chevigny ran well to set up Billy Dew's 4-yard TD. The final score ended up 26-7.

The Irish ran into one of the all-time greats when they played Minnesota—Bronko Nagurski, fortunately at guard in this game. But the Gophers also had Herb Joesting at fullback. With these two bruisers, this was a formidable team. Early in the game, Clipper Smith fell on a Gopher fumble, leading directly to Niemiec's score from their 18 on the next play. For three quarters, the scored stayed at 7-0, as two good defenses kept Flanagan and Joesting in check, respectively. Near the end of the game, with Niemiec in punt formation, the Irish were told they had 15 seconds left in the game. Riley checked off to a line plunge, in order to kill the clock and end the game, but somebody missed the call and the ball was snapped into the middle of the confused backfield. Nagurski fell on the ball. The time must not have been 15 seconds, because Minnesota had time for three Joesting runs and a scoring pass. The PAT kick was good and the Irish mistake cost

Christian Keener Cagle, one of the premier backs in Army football history.

them the game. One more time, Rockne's defense played with pluck and courage, but the offense showed that it was not able to dominate. In this game, they had real difficulty running up the middle, but Nagurski's brilliant, gutty play had much to do with that.

The Notre Dame-Army game was played in Yankee Stadium before more than 65,000 people. The Cadets were led by Christian Keener Cagle, one of the great backs in Army football annals. The ineffective Irish offense that had sputtered along all season haunted them throughout this game, an 18-0 losing effort, as Cagle scored on a 48-yard run and a 32-yard pass. Billy Nave, a very small back, caught Rockne's attention with an interception and 60-yard TD runback. A Rockne-led team had seldom been handled so easily … and Rockne knew that many of these Cadets would return for more of the same in the next campaign.

Drake took the brunt of Irish frustrations, 32-0. Rockne used the game to tune up his off-tackle plays and the passing game, and he also did what he could to rest the starters, saving them for the next game, USC's first visit to the midwest to play a Notre Dame team. Jack Elder, one of the fastest players ever to play for Rockne, intercepted a Drake pass and sped 80 yards to paydirt. Elder also fired a TD pass to John Colrick. Other Irish players to score were Niemiec, Dahman, and Joe Prelli.

The official record book lists 120,000 as the crowd for the 1927 USC game in Soldier Field, but the SRO crowd, jamming the place far beyond its capacity, likely reached the astounding figure of 135,000—probably the largest attendance at a sporting event in North America. These fortunates witnessed one of the great games ever; only in its second game, this series was already showing why it would regularly offer a classic contest. Bucky

Rockne in an ad for Studebaker made in South Bend. They would later name a model after the coach.

Dahman was easily the man-on-the-spot in front of this huge throng. He basically won the game: he caught a 25-yard TD pass from Riley, kicked the PAT, kicked a fourth quarter 65-yard punt that put the Trojans at their own 2, and later intercepted a USC pass on their 20 in the game's waning moments. With the final score being 7-6, Dahman's contributions were immense.

Flanagan and Clipper Smith made first team All-American teams; tackle John Polisky won second team honors. That was the season's good news. The bad news was that in nine games, Rockne's offense could only muster 158 points … and some of those were contributed by defensive play. It was Notre Dame's worst scoring output since the disastrous 1918 season. Rockne must have recognized that he and his team had been lucky to avoid major injuries in the 1927 season. They would not find the luck o' the Irish running their way in 1928.

January 1928 found Rockne back in his favorite city, New York, giving an "inspirational talk" to dealers of the Graham-Paige Motor Car Company. Paul Castner somehow learned of this (he does not mention having been there to hear Rockne's talk in person) and recommended Rockne to the Studebaker

Rockne gets Babe Ruth to give
it the old college try.

Ruth, Gehrig and other
Rockne cronies.

Corporation (headquartered in South Bend...why no one thought of this earlier is inexplicable). The vice president for sales in Studebaker, Paul Hoffman, quickly realized the potential for Rockne's success in exhorting Studebaker's dealers to improve their sales. Rockne signed a personal services contract on May 1 for a salary of $5000. He would give twenty-one talks before Studebaker dealers from January to March, 1929. An injury suffered in the 1929 football season kept him from giving any such talks during his second contract. He gave fourteen talks during his third and final contract before his untimely death. Sperber's book lists Rockne's total annual income during this period as $75,000—an amazing figure for the time, far beyond the income of his peers in the coaching business, roughly comparable to Babe Ruth's salary (the first pro athlete to earn more than the President of the United States). So, we can see that Rockne's rather belated relationship with Studebaker is part of his effort to capitalize on his growing fame.

Castner later wrote a book that contains the text of one of Rockne's inspirational talks, given to a Studebaker dealers' convention in Detroit on January 20, 1931, about two months before his death. Combined with the several examples of film taken with a sound track of Rockne's speaking style (and pep talk style), we can gain a rough sense of how the man delivered his goods: Rockne had a rather high-pitched voice, with a certain metallic quality to it, a slight nasality, with an idiosyncratic habit of raising the inflection at the end of an utterance so that the sentence final position seemed to be uplifted. His listeners found this unusual manner of speaking extremely effective, especially so for creating a sense of anticipation among those in his audience. By all accounts, it was a dynamic delivery—marked by what many people reported as a machine-gun-like rapid-fire delivery.

The Detroit speech, like almost everything Rockne wrote or said, was marked throughout by his brand of

(Above) Rockne, agent Christy Walsh, Pop Warner, in 1928 Paris.
(Below) Rockne and tennis star Bill Tilden.

humor. He liked to string together some football anecdotes designed to demonstrate various facets of psychology that Rockne thought would also apply in the business world. For him, the psychology that leads to success in football also is likely to create success in any organization, especially one involving salesmanship. Rockne spoke movingly of an early-season message about ambition that he would emphasize with each team at Notre Dame—the ambition to co-operate with all of one's teammates. Cooperation, Rockne claimed, is more important than technique. He directed the lesson to his Studebaker audience—car salesmen must know about the entire process of auto production and all the departments of the big corporation. Failure at any single point can cause failure throughout the company.

Rockne freely admitted to his listeners that he had never sold a car in his life. But he knew how to make his audience listen on his terms, as members of his "team." He spun tales about Gipp and the Four Horsemen, then concluded with what seems to be a self-parody of a locker room pep talk, a frenetic, half-shouted call for players to "go inside of 'em and outside of 'em—inside of 'em and outside of 'em—that's when we charge down the field—that's when we go! Go! Go!"

His players had heard this before on many occasions. The results on the playing field were manifest—numerous All-Americans, national championships, a Rose Bowl win, fame beyond imagination. And here he was doing the rah-rah thing for middle-aged salesmen. He had said almost nothing concrete about selling cars but, by all accounts, his message on team play, cooperation, and ambition was always driven home. Listeners in the audience must have feeling something like John Fogarty's line, "Put me in, coach!

I'm ready to play!"

Success in such endeavors led Rockne's many friends and associates to wonder if he would ever leave coaching to throw himself into the business world. The jury was split; some thought he was always on the lookout for a good opportunity. There is some merit in this view; as we know, Rockne did flirt with other schools and was conscious of achieving a measure of security for his family. He was also proficient in setting up a series of coaching clinics and generally had the good sense to follow up on his increasing name recognition with his books, Olympic tour, articles, and the like.

On the other hand, his experience at the Post Office had probably been enough to cure him forever of fitting into a bureaucratic mold, without significant room for self-expression and personal ingenuity. He might well have been totally out of his element in the business world. At Notre Dame, he was pretty much a one-man force for his vision of athletics and football. He had an enormous field to play in; he did have to answer to various committees, but even then football was more or less a power unto itself. He had tremendous leverage and knew how to use it. His advice to Studebaker salesmen may have had general applicability, but he was not generously endowed with business acumen, as he learned in the Columbia contract affair and as he had occasion to back off when in conflict with senior administrators at Notre Dame. Finally, he seems to have been a bit of a thrill junkie; one wonders if the business world would have been able to provide the intensity of a pressure-packed fourth quarter goalline stand, or the sheer excitement of a long-distance TD on a perfect play. In sum, it is likely that he would have stayed with the status quo—lots of football and income earned from name recognition. He died so young that had he stayed at Notre Dame for the full career, he would have been the coach to recruit a youngster from Kentucky named Paul Hornung. We cannot ever be certain that he would have stayed that long (very few head coaches do...one's welcome wears out eventually, or the pressures become less acceptable as one goes through life). But to think of Knute Rockne at Notre Dame through a second World War and into the early 1950s is one

Shipboard, headed for the 1928
Amsterdam Olympics.

Paul Hornung

Rockne and UND alumni president,
John Neeson.

The 1928 coaching staff faced major challenges.

way of considering what did not take place in collegiate football as a result of his untimely loss.

Some seasons in college football are living examples of the pertinence of Murphy's Law ... if the worst can happen, it will. That Murphy might have been of Irish extraction is no consolation when the worst happens to the Notre Dame football team. The 1928 season proved to be one of these worst case scenarios, but with all the adversity it would be the occasion for one of the sporting world's most famous stories.

Like the 1921 season, sandwiched between Gipp and the Four Horsemen, the 1928 squad followed the stability of the three Flanagan-led seasons with no sign of a dominant star or unit. There were some good veteran backs—Chevigny, Niemiec, and Elder were solid as halfbacks, while Collins and Moon Mullins provided dependable fullbacks. In this group, Rockne would have to worry about avoiding injuries; there were some knee problems here. Rockne would be searching among the sophomores to find some leadership on the offense.

The opener was against Loyola of New Orleans. The Wolfpack managed to stake itself to a 6-0 lead, but Jack Elder turned on the jets for a 48-yard TD run. Neither team could do much afer that. Rockne's sixth sense for changing a game's pace alerted him late in the game—so he put in a pair of young receivers, Johnny O'Brien and Tom Murphy. Niemiec hit O'Brien with a long pass, the play reaching Loyola's 8 yard line. Two plays later, Niemiec scored the winning TD on an off-tackle

Halfback Jack Chevigny

play from the 2.

Against Wisconsin, Rockne had to be mortified to see ND lose seven fumbles, along with the game, 22-6. One of the fumbles went over to Wisconsin at the Irish 3. Surprisingly, Elder, speedy though he was, was trapped for a safety; Chevigny scored a consolation TD for the Irish.

Rockne must have known by now that this team was a threat to lose any game it was playing. Ever the master of motivation, he tried something against Navy that another Irish head coach (Dan Devine, a four-year-old at the time of this game) would use at a crucial moment against USC—put the Irish in Kelly green uniforms. He also eschewed his shock troops tactic, playing his starters virtually the whole game. The Irish won the game in the fourth quarter when Niemiec fired a sharp pass to Colrick on a slant pattern for the game's only TD. ND won the

The 1928 team leaving for the Navy game.

game 7-0 as more than 120,000 fans watched a great defensive effort that held Navy to 93 total yards.

Nothing much seemed to work at all as Notre Dame fell to Georgia Tech 13-0. Tech intercepted two Irish passes and revealed a serious weakness in the Notre Dame offense when they easily stopped a series of line smashes by the Irish fullbacks deep in the red zone. After this, Rockne tried to improve the situation at fullback by moving Mullins to starter. Thus fortified, ND managed a 32-6 victory over Drake. The scoring was spread around, with two notable items emerging—center Joe Nash rumbled 50 yards for a TD with an interception, and sophomore QB Frank Carideo, a name to remember, slogged through some desultory tacklers for a TD. Mullins did not score, but he played a courageous game at fullback.

The Irish played a pretty good game against Penn State; things were looking up...unless you were Rockne, who was perfectly cognizant of this team's limitations. The score here was a modest 9-0. Rules were different then, so don't be alarmed to learn that Carideo crawled into the endzone—under and through the Nittany Lions—for the one Irish TD. Colrick's speed created a safety in the fourth quarter. Eddie Collins had a great series—tackling a Penn State runner for a twenty-yard loss, then recovering a fumble on the next play.

Just past the mid-point of the season, the Irish stood at 4-2, only the third time in eleven seasons under Rockne that they had two losses. There was every likelihood that it would get worse, Rockne mused. Facing a powerful Army team, he knew that the Irish would have to win this game to avert the possibility of a losing season. The team had its limitations and was probably putting out as much effort as it could, given those limitations. He had already used the Kelly green trick earlier in the season...what else might come in handy? He was known to fib to his players..."Win one for my little sick boy back home" and the like. He could call on all the echoes with the best of them. But he needed more than a color, a sick child, or heroic echoes. He needed the kind of player he didn't have. Rockne was pretty good at cutting a variety of corners, quite willing and able. But he couldn't put in

The starting eleven for the difficult 1928 campaign.

a ringer; he couldn't flat out cheat.

Not really. But he claimed later to have told Grantland Rice the night before the game that he might have to use the ghost of George Gipp against Army. We have already discussed earlier what Gipp might or might not have said to Rockne as he neared death in 1920. Whether Gipp said anything at all is one of those imponderables. We do know, however, that Rockne certainly used words that he attributed to Gipp at the halftime of the 1928 Army game, to provide that last little milligram of incentive and motivation for a team that was really doing all it could with what it had. Coaches cannot justifiably demand more than a team is capable of giving—but they can supply the seed that grows into something more to give. Furthermore, Rockne waited until the last possible moment to play his ace. In a situation like this, as William Shakespeare knew, ripeness is all. He could have completely wasted it earlier in the year, not fully knowing what his team could give him, or not having the big picture yet on the season's opponents. It could also be misused if broached too early in a given contest; athletes can only sustain a burst of inspiration for so long. So, he had to get it right. He only had one chance to use his Gipp story (true or false, but that's not the point here) and there was precious little margin for error. It would have to be either before the game or at the halftime—there's little chance in a football game to do it at any other time, because hell's a poppin' all around a coach as he prowls a sideline area. If there was a need to call on Gipp's memory, that is, if the Irish were still in the game, logically it would have to be at halftime.

Army had a loaded team built around the great Chris Cagle. They were big (except for Nave) and experienced. But the Irish defense early in the game learned that they could play with the Cadets, without being manhandled, and could neutralize Cagle. The first half was a 0-0 struggle, both teams unable to make a serious dent in the other's armor, although ND managed a drive to the Army 2-yard line that ended with a fumble recovered for a touchback. Both teams were giving it their best, as usual in this series at the time.

In the halftime Irish locker room, we'd expect to see the usual scene—fatigued, grimy players, many with various injuries being attended to, the starters mulling over the game's events and the guy they had faced repeatedly for the first half, veterans giving tips to younger players, the assistant coaches in little clusters with the players they worked with most. Then a command, Rockne's gravel voice, the players raise their heads, all eyes on him. We know the rest, or think we do, from his accounts, from film, from books and newspapers.

He told them the story of Gipp and the supposed deathbed request—to "Win One for the Gipper!" These players surely knew of Gipp, at least the official,

Babe Ruth with Knute Rockne.

cleaned-up version, and certainly they all had a sense of the tragic waste of a superb athlete taken in his prime, of the wretched waste of human potential. They surely stood in awe of Gipp's football exploits, most of which would last in the Irish record books for six decades after he died.

So, here they were, deep in the bowels of Yankee Stadium (Ruth had hammered his 60 homers in one season just the year before), playing one of the storied teams of college football, in the presence of a coach who was well on his way to football immortality, in the middle of a great game … and Rockne lays this on them. They could have folded their collective tents right then (unlikely for a Rockne-coached team), or over-reacted by leaving the locker room and expending their energies frenetically. But Rockne got it right—they were able to sustain a superb effort in the second half, overcoming Army's excellent play and Cagle's brilliant heroics.

Cagle lived up to his star billing. He started out the second half with a 20-yard gain, then threw a 41-yard pass to set up a TD and Army's 6-0 lead. He also kept busy on defense. The Irish managed to put together a scoring drive in response, Chevigny scoring on a fourth-down plunge, reportedly exulting, "That's one for the Gipper!" Shortly after that, however, Chevigny was injured in recovering a fumble and taken from the game. Rockne inserted Johnny O'Brien; with that substitution, Niemiec knew what to do. With the ball snapped to him, Niemiec drifted back to pass but mainly saw Army pass rushers headed his way. He heaved the ball in the general

Johnny "One-Play" O'Brien
caught the winning TD pass against Army in 1928 from
Niemiec.

direction of O'Brien, who was being defended by one of the heroes of the '27 Army win—Billy Nave. But Nave was badly overmatched, giving away seven inches or more to the lanky O'Brien. It wasn't a thing of beauty, this pass, nor the catch—O'Brien grabbing the ball, stumbling almost backwards over the futile effort of Nave. Still, it worked for the TD and a 12-6 Irish lead.

But Army wasn't done yet. Chris Cagle returned the kickoff to the Irish 31, then led his team all the way to the ND 10. But Cagle had seen his last play in the game at that crucial place on the field. Totally exhausted, he was taken from the game. Both teams had thus lost key players at crucial points—Chevigny for the Irish earlier and now Cagle. Army was a gritty, determined team, but they didn't have Gipp working on their behalf. The Cadets drove to the Irish one-yard line but the referee, none other than Rockne's close friend Walter Eckersall, blew the whistle to end the game. Ed "Moose" Krause, ND's longtime Athletic Director, who knew most of the principal Irish personnel involved in the game's last few plays and seconds, noted years later that the desperate goal-line defense stopped Army and the Irish held possession of the ball at their own 1 yard line. Army partisans have

A pass to Fred Collins in the great 1928 game with Army.

Left half John Niemiec drops back to pass against Army in 1928.

argued otherwise for years. Perhaps Gipp was somehow involved in the game-saving tackle...we'll never know.

Rockne's brilliant ploy had worked. Like an athlete in some marathon event, he necessarily had to gauge the energy level and general prospects of his charges. He surely wanted to avoid a losing season. Just another barn-burning halftime speech wouldn't do it. He had to use the right approach at the right time. With that done, no one should be surprised that the Irish would find it difficult to duplicate their defeat of a superior Army team.

Carnegie Tech pounced on a vulnerable ND team a week later, humbling the Irish 27-7. Tech had a 230-pound fullback named Karcis and he hammered the small Irish linemen without mercy. The only Irish score came on a fumble recovery by Mullins. Prior to this disappointment, Notre Dame had not lost a home game since Rockne had been a senior in high school—1905.

Out on the west coast, Notre Dame met USC for its 300th football game. The Trojans won the game 27-14, but the Irish did not go down easily. Chevigny made his mark with a 51-yard TD run, and Albie Gebert, subbing at QB, tallied the other. At one point in the game, a bone-weary but proud Irish defense made USC come away empty four times from the ND 4-yard line to frustrate a long Trojan drive.

In the decade in which Rockne had led Irish football fortunes, it seems that anything that could happen did happen. Most of it was good and right, but some of it was sad and lamentable. He managed to get through it all without letting it crush him. Surely Rockne was singularly responsible for launching Notre Dame football into the prominence it currently enjoys—which also means that he was partially but directly the cause of the tremendous pressures encountered by anyone who holds the job of Notre Dame's head football coach. His team had been undefeated in 1919, 1920, and 1924. He had produced numerous All-Americans and had seen one of them become a virtual icon of American football history and culture. An entire backfield had become a household word (well, words). The name and face of Knute Rockne were known everywhere in America. Notre Dame was at the forefront of American colleges in terms of name recognition—and would use that fame to launch itself into the highest echelons of the world's universities. Rockne had made an indelible impression upon the game of football—its tactics, its equipment, its color and dash, its rules. He had turned 40 in 1928. He did not know it, but

Rockne coaching in his usual style.

he was in the final decade of his life, a life that had obviously wildly outstripped whatever promise it had in Voss.

Unbelievably, there was much more to happen.

The tremendous growth in America of college football, and the changes that accompanied that growth, led to what came to be called "the overemphasis issue." That is, critics of the game were alarmed that it threatened the integrity of the academic purposes and pursuits at the country's institutions of higher education. They recalled with great nostalgia the days before "coaches" were hired to lead teams—a feature of the game's development that emerged as the early generations of players produced a large body of former players who had the minimal expertise deemed necessary to guide a team's football fortunes. In those days, student managers were the important operative figures in arranging schedules and handling whatever finances were involved. Team captains were entrusted with conditioning, practices, setting up training tables, defining the starting team, and planning for game strategy. This was the state of affairs at Notre Dame, for instance, in the five "seasons" played between 1887 and 1893; the first football coach, James L. Morison, who had played his college football as a tackle at Michigan, was hired in 1894. The players of the time still exercised a large degree of control even in such decisions.

All this changed inexorably as "coaches" took on greater prominence in the various aspects of the game. It is to be expected that they would want to exercise a higher degree of control over their teams and their own career fates. This is precisely what they did. During this transition period, roughly from 1890 to 1910, the problem of "football tramps" took on significant proportions. Football tramps were those who managed to play college football far beyond the four years now deemed standard. These men bounced from school to school—record keeping then was a minimal, spotty affair—and were able to cobble together playing careers that might last seven and eight, or more, seasons. Maintaining one's academic eligibility was unheard of. Early coaches were more or less temporary phenomena and often had almost no significant connection to a college's senior administration. Obviously, such a state of affairs was rife with possibilities for abuse.

A major factor in this scene has to be sheer economics. The role played by money is found everywhere: bets between teams, money needed for equipment and travel, managing the finances based on game receipts, salaries for the coach (and later his staff), stipends for game officials, the major investments represented by early, primitive playing facilities, but also money passed under the table for the players to help defer their own expenses as students. The possibilities for a variety of abuses in this situation were enormous. Eventually, football teams and athletic departments became virtual separate empires adjacent to, and sometimes within, existing collegiate administrative structures. To the critics, this all smacked of a low-life form of "professionalism" that shattered the amateur ideal (although a compelling case can be made that this ideal had never existed but operated primarily as a myth). Other than Walter Camp's rules committee, there was no recognized organization that could oversee this complex, evolving state of affairs. It is significant that it took the intervention of a U.S. president, Teddy Roosevelt, to bring together key figures after the 1905 season for the simple matter of changing the rules to allow for the forward pass to be legalized.

Ultimately, however, the critics of college football were motivated by the pervasive mind-body split that has been a feature of Western attitudes toward the life of the mind and the life of the body since the Greek Olympics of 2,500 years ago. In general, the mind has been perceived as the higher value; the needs of the body have been perceived as gross and appetitive. The two exist more or less in conflict, with the body's needs serving to drain the mind of its salutary strengths. In religious terms, the body has often been seen as the evil partner threatening the salvation of the person's soul—a strong factor in the developing history of America, with its Puritanical roots. (One wonders about the state of those pristine collegiate minds when we learn that the library at such prestigious universities as Princeton, in 1868, was open to undergraduate use one hour per week—or nearby Rutgers where students could access library books only from 8:30 am to 9:00 am each Saturday of the academic year. Nostalgia for a lost, innocent past, or a past that simply never was, largely helps account for this). That major American sports were in a clear take-off stage at roughly the same time as the demise of classical learning in the 1890s (as vernacular literature replaced Latin and Greek, for instance) is both neither an accident nor something that critics from an elitist perspective could support. For better or worse, intercollegiate athletics represented a significant

One of the most famous faces in the Golden Age of Sport in the Twenties.

component of an early wave of the democratization of American higher education. Friendly participation in a variety of sports had been a common experience among the millions of soldiers who fought in the Civil War (which may help account partially for the long-standing relationship of American sports and war and the military); that their children and grandchildren would continue the trend a generation later is no surprise.

Rockne arrived at Notre Dame in the Fall of 1910 just as the various strands of this convoluted phenomenon were playing out at Notre Dame. Red Salmon's senior season, 1903, was probably the last season when a team captain at Notre Dame had a major, definitive say in how things operated for the team. The last possible Irish "tramp players" may have just completed the 1909 season—Ralph Dimmick and George Philbrook both attracted Fielding Yost's attention and suspicions due to their years spent playing college football in the Pacific Northwest, leading to his protests over Michigan's loss to the 1909 ND team and subsequent refusal to continue the series for more than thirty years, factors also abetted by his dislike of Catholics. Notre Dame's head coaches had all been temporary figures on the campus scene. Of the twelve head coaches prior to Harper in 1913, only one had served as many as three years; all the others coached only one or two seasons before moving on. Harper stayed for five seasons and Rockne would last for thirteen, before his untimely death forced a change.

The critics of the game also complained about the matter of concentrating the resources of the colleges for the benefit of the elite few (who did not, in their view, need enhanced physical benefits) rather than sharing the resources for the general good of the student body; inculcating incorrect values by emphasizing athletic excellence over academic excellence; sports' contributing to the moral delinquency of the student body through the introduction of increased opportunities for gambling, drinking (!!), and other features of loose living; the winning ethic displacing a better-balanced approach to games; and general matters relating to the intrusion of the marketplace in the academy (as if boards of trustees and curricula were unrelated to the marketplace). The specific charges of the critics included recruiting violations, anti-intellectualism, slush funds, spring practices, and exorbitant indebtedness for stadiums.

The critics also expressed concern that the sport was growing so quickly that immediate action was necessary to stem the tide. They looked fondly to an academic past when a college's cocurricular events did not include mass sports. The presidents and many faculty members of the leading institutions had entered their academic careers when intercollegiate sports were rare events, when it was unthinkable that a nonfaculty coach could have a salary in excess of the school president's salary. The war years led to fairly quiet campus life for administrators in 1917-1918, but whatever hopes for this state to continue were dashed when the American Army, the AEF, held a massive sports spectacle between its many divisions just prior to demobilization in 1919.

The returning veterans brought to colleges their pent-up enthusiasm for intercollegiate athletics and football in particular. The brief respite from the rapid increase in the popularity of the game turned, instead, to greater support after football came to be seen as a socially valuable vehicle for the promotion of physical fitness and as an appropriate prep for combat. Americans were appalled by the numbers of young men deemd to be unfit for military service. This became one of the leading rationales for increasing institutional support for athletic programs. Whereas football was not seen prior to the war as a socially useful sport, it now began to take on that aura. Before the war, about all the supporters of football could muster in support of the game was that it produced splendid physical examples of manhood. This was not enough for college administrations. In 1916, Yale severely curtailed intercollegiate athletics, a premature move in light of postwar attitudes. Unable to make inroads by trying to abolish football or radically reducing programs, critics changed their tactics to argue the issue of overemphasis.

Rockne was highly instrumental in defending the game of football against this attack. He took his cue from former University of Notre Dame President Father Andrew Morrissey who, at the turn of the century, rejected the narrow view that the university's sole task was to educate the mind alone. Morrissey articulated the view that "education of the head at the expense of the heart" was a major problem of the day. He landed firmly on the side of the proposition that athletics have a positive function. He seems to have set the tone that Notre Dame has followed ever since, one for which Rockne became the embodiment at the national level.

The bust of Knute Rockne in the
Notre Dame building named for him.

For Rockne, football was not distinct from other aspects of life. He perceived direct correlations between the values engendered in the game and those needed to succeed in life. He felt that the critics of football were operating in a hypothetical realm, blind to the real benefits of the game for those who participated in it. His greatest ire was reserved for those who took the fun out of the game—unethical, humorless alumni and big-time gamblers, both of whom created unnecessary pressures around the game. (He appears not to have been too concerned with the low-level betting that surrounded players like Gipp, whose career preceded the overemphasis issue).

In this debate, Rockne placed tremendous value on the joyful, pristine nature of sport, minimizing the negative factors. He was not blind to abuses, reserving particular scorn for coaches who exploited players in any way. For him, the coach must establish and meet high standards for his sense of right living and fair play. Sportsmanship, the football version of the Golden Rule, he found to be the basis for an entire philosophy of life, applicable on the field of play, in interpersonal matters, even in the international arena.

The starting eleven for the 1929
National Champs. They never
played a home game.

The final chapter to the saga of this Norwegian hero begins with the 1929 Notre Dame football team. All sports teams are always evolving, and in college football this is brutally obvious in the fact of having players for only three seasons (at the time) over four years. Under those circumstances, a team's stability in terms of personnel turnover is always fragile. Professional football teams have their cycles, too, but they are longer ... taking place over much of a decade or longer, perhaps. In the college game, a team's character can change almost overnight. Two seasons can be a sea change.

The 1929 team was, like a couple of others in Rockne's years, a transitional team. The line was a solid, mature group; the backfield had both speed and pretty good size (you can see Rockne's recruiting results changing away from the pony backfield of 1924 to a much larger, more physical backfield by the end of the decade—due largely to the rules changes that eventually nullified the backfield shift). Rockne's quarterback would be Frank Carideo, a fiery leader from the east, with a brilliant supporting backfield cast—Marchy Schwartz from New Orleans at right half, Jack Elder's blazing speed at left halfback, with Marty Brill, a Penn transfer in the wings, and Mullins at fullback, with a rugged throwback type, Joe Savoldi, subbing there.

Rockne had pioneered the so-called "suicide" schedule, a season with a minimum number of patsies, then he added the coast-to-coast schedule (all the more impressive before jet travel). The 1929 season would witness an innovation few head coaches would risk—no home games. All the games were on the road (some fairly near to ND) because Cartier Field had pretty much outlived its usefulness. Early season crowds would only reach 10,000 or so...big home games would hit 27,000. The field had minimal amenities. The Irish had been treated to the big venues in New York, the new LA Coliseum, the Rose Bowl, and had seen 120,000+ in Soldier Field. The gates at those sites must have made Rockne's head swim. With Notre Dame's fame and fandom on the rise almost exponentially, it made perfect sense to try to capture the potential gate for home games. The University of Michigan had been the first college to play the fledgling Irish, in 1887; forty years later, Michigan's newly erected stadium would serve as the model for the proposed Notre Dame stadium.

As a coach and tactician, Rockne had already shown a keen eye for the minute details of football. He had opened up the game for its mass spectacle appeal. (One wonders if the old style of the game had been at all

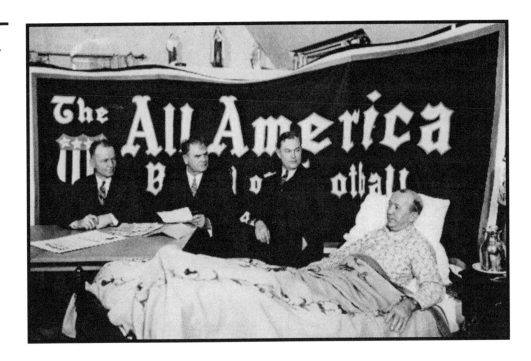

Injured in the 1929 Indiana game, Rockne attempted to keep up his pace, meeting here with his All-American committee.

confusing to the mind and eye of the young Norwegian). He had made it brighter and literally more eye-pleasing. It was a more democratic game, in many respects, due to his influence. Note the pattern here—from this litany we can note that Rockne was a very visually oriented person, one who could see things quite well from the perspective of others, find them deficient in some way, and then go about changing the paradigm so as to make it an improved product.

Well, at the end of the 1920s, Rockne seems to have had in mind what would become the ultimate way of "seeing" for the last half of the century—television. The stadium project he oversaw gave ND a small jewel of a stadium, with excellent sight lines, very close proximity to the field of play, and excellent acoustics to augment a crowd's excitement or the band's playing. He attended to other matters as well, such as the parking arrangements, and the choice of materials for the stadium's seating. That basic stadium would last Notre Dame for years, including a stretch of sell-outs from the mid-1970's until the completion of the renovation in 1997-1998.

The first game of the 1929 season was at Indiana. The subs played well enough to keep the Hoosiers from mounting any serious threats. For youngsters, Savoldi and Schwartz showed some flashes of talent. Elder, one of the fastest sprinters in the world at the time, scooted for a 20-yard TD, after setting the stage with a pass to Mullins. He also tallied the game's other score with a 60-yard TD burst. Irish errors, chiefly fumbles, kept the team from adding to the 14-0 final score. But the game was more important for something that happened off the field of play when it was marred by a sideline pileup engulfing Rockne—three players hit him more or less simultaneously. The trauma to his legs led to acute phlebitis setting in. Rockne's activities were severely curtailed, much to his chagrin. He would remain under almost constant medical care for the rest of the season, miss many practices—even some games, and have his cardiopulmonary condition and general movement scrupulously monitored. Assistant coach Tom Lieb, who played on ND's varsity in 1921-1922, took over the day-to-day care and handling of the team.

In the week intervening between the Indiana and Navy games, Rockne arranged for his quarterbacks to visit him, bed-ridden, in his house, not too far from the campus. In sessions running a bit more than two-and-a-half hours, Rockne put his QBs through the paces with a rapid-fire Q & A session, stating offensive and defensive game situations and looking for the best response to each. He made a point of speaking to each starter on the phone before the game, which was in Baltimore, to encourage them and reassure them about his condition. Having been physically involved in Notre Dame football since 1910, it had to be excruciating for him to listen passively to game accounts from the radio. Missing the Navy game this way had to be worse than his Carnegie Tech fiasco of 1926.

When Navy jumped out to a 7-0 lead, Rockne must have had a sinking feeling. There was nothing he could do but sit it out at home and hope for the best. But Carideo got the Irish moving and soon hit Elder with a TD pass thrown from one knee (remember the different rules then) after he had taken a glancing hit. Carideo made a big difference on defense as well, attesting to the quality of Rockne's bedside coaching. The quarterback intercepted a Middie pass and returned it to their 32. Brill contributed runs of 7 and 17 yards, setting up a one-yard TD plunge by Mullins, sealing a 14-7 Notre Dame victory.

Rockne's physician knew he would be a difficult patient. He had never really known or admitted to personal limits. He had coached in a vigorous way, often mixing it up physically with his players in practices. All this was lost. Had his trauma occurred today, he would have a wide array of therapeutic and rehabilitative practices. At the time, he was a close friend of the family that operated the McGann funeral home in South Bend. They arranged to loan him one of their hearses. So, Rockne would be trundled into a wheelchair, wrapped in blankets, and more or less shoved into the hearse. Taken to the practice field, allowed to rest outside the hearse, Rockne could see that the week's practices were going well. He communicated via a microphone and loudspeaker arrangement. Surely, the players were not going to disappoint him; he was living proof of how to be tough and get the job done in spite of personal obstacles and seeming limitations.

Against Wisconsin, Rockne's charges executed a workmanlike shutout, 19-0. Led by Joe Savoldi's TD runs from 40 and 71 yards out (keep in mind that he was a 200-pound fullback), and Elder's 43-yard sprint, the Irish gave Rockne another get well win, a 19-0 triumph over the Badgers.

Their coach kept plugging away at his duties, in considerable pain and discomfort all the while. Carnegie Tech was the next opponent, and they still had Karcis at fullback. Tech's 1928 win had interrupted an Irish winning streak at home that had begun before most of the 1929 players were born. Once again, Tech was not going to be a pushover. Rockne knew this. Prior to the game, he arranged to have Tom Lieb carry him into the Irish dressing room, a pathetic sight given the experience his players had of him. The team had been sitting there waiting, waiting—for whatever. And then Rockne comes in, a babe in Lieb's arms. Lieb gently placed Rockne on the training table in the locker room. Rockne sat there, unmoving, quiet ... for five minutes. He let the emotion and tension in the room become palpable. A physician in the room, Dr. Maurice Keady, leaned over and spoke to Francis Wallace. In his estimation, if Rockne became too animated, if he "lets go," the clot in his leg could dislodge and enter his heart or brain. If that happened, Dr. Keady gave Rockne a 50-50 chance of leaving the room

Rockne waited; usually given to talking, his being quiet must have signified something portentious to his assembled men. When he did start talking, he mentioned all the crises he had encountered in his decades at Notre Dame. Many of these players had heard his Yankee Stadium Gipper speech at the end of the prior season—indeed, less than a year before. Maybe they were a bit jaded with these entreaties (but probably not). He got their attention for sure when he told them, as recorded by Francis Wallace, that he never wanted to win a game as badly as this one. He was aware that he was taking a big chance … they wouldn't want to lose would they? He reviewed the strengths of Carnegie Tech. The Irish wouldn't want to lose to them again, would they? Wallace saw his face taking on a grim look. His voice rising, he implored his team to "Fight to win. Fight to live. Fight to win—win—WIN!" His players charged out of the room to the field. Rockne slumped on the training table, drained, emptied. God only knows what catharsis he had gone through, what was purged from his system. In any case, Wallace concluded that the man wanted to win more than he wanted to live. Surely Rockne must have considered what he was doing, weighing the possibilities—his health, life, his family—against a football game.

The Gipper speech is more famous, to be sure. Perhaps other motivational methods and incidents come to mind readily when we think of Rockne. But this example shows how single-minded the man was when it came to forcing his will on his own better inclinations. He basically risked it all—health, life, family—for a football game. He had to have given it some thought, pondered the possibilities. He was from a family of risk-takers. He had a fairly clear track record of taking risks, but he also had done his homework on risk assessment. It surely seems though that his competitive zeal got the better of his sound judgment. Fighting to live, in his own words, is preferable to fighting to the death. Did he contradict himself? Or was this his own way of living out his own words? We may never know, but we can readily see how Rockne personified the dramatic, flamboyant romantic strain that char-

Handsome Jack Cannon somehow maintained his good loks without wearing a helmet for the Irish—the last man to do so.

acterized the Twenties as a whole.

Rockne's histrionics did not galvanize the team this time. In the middle of the third quarter, the game was scoreless. Carideo finally got the Irish moving with a punt return to midfield, followed shortly by a 35-yard Elder run to the Tech 17. Brill hauled it to the 8. Savoldi came in...big fullback on big fullback, as the game was played then. Three times Savoldi powered into the Carnegie Tech line, with Karcis holding him at bay. Finally, insistently, on fourth down, Savoldi finished his work with a TD, the winning score in a 7-0 squeaker. In retrospect, it may be that Rockne's pre-game appeal might have sapped his player's emotional reserves rather than stoking them.

Georgia Tech served as hosts for Rockne's Ramblers next—a formidable opponent given their defending national champ status. They came out of the gates fast, grabbing a fumble by Mullins at the ND 19 for an early 6-0 lead. The Irish struck back quickly—Brill zipped with the kickoff to the ND 40...Elder zoomed 53 yards with nary a scratch for what amounted to the game's go-ahead TD. In a subsequent series, surely a record of some dubious sort was set by Domer Jack Cannon—the last man to play football for the Irish *sans* head gear. He managed to block a Georgia Tech punt with his noggin, Mullins picked up the loose ball, and the Irish were in business again with a 13-6 halftime lead. Rockne always preached using one's head in football, but this is probably not exactly what he had in mind. In the second half, Carideo showed his leadership as Rockne's QB by skittering 75 yards for a TD with a punt return. In the fourth quarter, Marchy Schwartz wrapped it up with an 8-yard TD burst for the 26-6 final score. Rockne's spirits and health were probably mending nicely after this.

For their second game of the season at Chicago's Soldier Field, the Irish faced Drake and showed once again how difficult it is to sustain a superlative effort. Drake scored first for a 7-0 lead, but ND took control for a 19-7 win. Al Howard scored on a short run, Elder streaked 17 yards for the second TD, and Mullins romped 23 yards for the last score. Rockne must have been feeling pretty chipper by now.

Enough so that he risked impairing his recovery by violating his doctor's orders to attend the USC game the next week, also played at Soldier Field. The 50,00 who had turned out for the Drake game became more than

Rockne's last captain—1930's Tom Conley.

112,000 for the USC contest, another good indication of the magnitude of what Rockne had set in motion with this intersectional series. The 1929 vintage proved to one of the all-time thrillers: USC went ahead on a TD pass over Bucky O'Connor...whose swollen black eye prevented his seeing the pass before it was too late. Shortly after this, Elder showed his impressive versatility with a 54-yard TD pass to Tom Conley to make it a 6-6 game. The next Irish score came largely upon the efforts of Savoldi, who primed a fierce running game on a TD drive, scored the second TD for the Irish and a 13-6 lead. The Trojan kick returner took the Irish kick back 92 yards for a return score, but they missed the conversion and lost the game to ND 13-12. One can only wonder how this barn-burner settled with Rockne, confined to his wheelchair, grumpy about his sedentary existence. In fact, it almost killed him, because that night a blood clot dislodged, according to Francis Wallace, went through his heart, missed his

brain and settled in his other leg. He had seen his last Notre Dame game for the season. This incident demonstrates quite well just how risky his behavior before the Carnegie Tech game had been.

Notre Dame next went to meet old rival Northwestern (nine games in forty years). Rockne remained behind, lucky to be alive after the effort expended in the USC game. He fibbed to the team by telling them that this would be his 100th win...and the players either didn't know his record or just took his word for granted. In any case, they whacked the Wildcats 26-6. The second quarter spelled doom for Northwestern— Schwartz started it with a 40-yard run to set up a Savoldi score. The Irish kept up

Frank Carideo, starting QB for the 1929-30 national champs.

the pressure with a pass from Schwartz to Brill good for 25 yards to the NU 10-yard line, then Schwartz hauled it in from there. Carideo must have felt left out of the fun, because he espied a Wildcat pass, intercepted it, and jetted 85 yards for another Irish TD. Savoldi wrapped it up with a 32-yard run to set up a TD plunge for the final score.

The season's last game was against Army and was played in Yankee Stadium. It was Chris Cagle's last game for the Cadets. The grand occasion was marred only by frozen turf that made footing treacherous for all players. In his pre-game telephone conversation with Tom Lieb, Rockne recommended that the Irish sharpen their cleats for better footing—a crucial piece of advice as it turned out. The teams played it conservatively for a good part of the game, more out of necessity than design. Eventually, Army made a break for itself when a Cadet put on a good

The end of an Irish record that may never be broken—Jack Elder's 100-yard interception for a touchdown in the 1929 Army game, the game's only score.

rush on a punt play, knocking Elder back into Carideo, the Irish punter. Army had the ball on the ND 13 and chose to try to jam it in from there, but two runs netted only 2 yards. Cagle then took the snap and dropped into a passing formation; he saw his end, Carlmark, open and fired the pass for a score … a Notre Dame score, because the alert Elder saw it coming and swooped into the scene at the perfect split second, picked the pass off cleanly, and ran gingerly down the icy right sideline for a 100-yard TD return (according to the observant Steve Boda's most recent statistical proclamation). Irish defenders kept up the pressure with three more interceptions to seal a crucial 7-0 victory.

The 1929 season saw Rockne's Irish play before 551,112 spectators, the first time an Irish team had performed for more than a half million people—a figure that would not be surpassed for nearly twenty seasons. Indeed, the 1929 figure matches the season attendance for the 1960-1963 seasons, as well as the 1969 and 1973 teams—the latter a national championship season for Parseghian. For George Gipp's last season, 1920, Notre Dame had played before a mere 89,000 people, little more than 78% of the people who witnessed the single Notre Dame game with USC in 1929. For the decade, Rockne's teams averaged 273,000 fans per season, although very large season figures from 1926-1929 inflate the figure dramatically.

Rockne's 1929 team won the Rissman Trophy, a national championship trophy awarded to the team with the most demanding schedule. His team had four shutouts, held four other teams to a touchdown or less, with only USC scoring in double digits in its epic 13-12 loss. The Irish scored 145 points to the opposition's mere 38, for an average score of 16 to 4, almost a two-TD margin. Quarterback Fred Carideo and the helmetless Jack Cannon were consensus All-Americans, with tackle Ted Twomey garnering second team status. (Rockne's teams had produced 26 All-Americans so far in his head coaching years at Notre Dame). This 1929 team had never played a home game and had to function without their inspiring head coach for six of their nine games, yet they managed to dominate in virtually every significant statistical category.

If the 1929 team was very good, the 1930 team Rockne put together was close to awesome. Whereas he had three All-Americans on the team in 1929, the line alone produced three All-Americans in 1930. The Irish backfield was probably the best physically, as a unit, ever in Irish football history to that point. With Carideo at quarterback, Rockne had an experienced, fearless, tough, charismatic leader. With Brill and Schwartz running as halfbacks, Rockne had two elusive, speedy, long-range scoring threats. Savoldi at fullback was a punishing runner who could also break loose for a long gainer. Rockne had not been sitting on his hands as those opposed to the shift kept nibbling away at it. Of course, he had the largest backfield he would ever coach in this 1930 unit. But he also added a series of spinners—plays in which the QB or the back the ball had been snapped to would spin around and handoff, or fake, or lateral as backs angled in near him. He could also roll out and pass after the fake. It looked very much like the Veer offense Ara Parseghian's teams would use in the 1970s. It was awfully tough to defend.

The first game of the 1930 season, also the first game to be played in the new stadium, was against Southern Methodist. The Mustangs were the BYU of their era—given almost exclusively to the passing game. They demonstrated this beautifully on their fourth play of the game, scoring on a 48-yard pass and run play. On the ensuing kickoff, the ball went to Savoldi, who promptly bobbled it, but recovered in time to turn on the jets for a 98-yard TD sprint. Schwartz scored on a short run in the second quarter and SMU's aerial assault worked for another TD and a 14-14 halftime score. It stayed that way well into the fourth quarter, when Schwartz zipped a pass to Ed Kosky for a 48-yard gain to the SMU 27. On the next play, the Ponies were hit with a pass interference call at their own 4. Schwartz took a handoff and ran a cutback past left end for the final score of 20-14. Tommy Yarr staved off further SMU damage with three interceptions.

The official dedication of the new stadium was set prior to the Navy game. After the ceremonies, the Irish showed how much they had improved (considering three close games with the Middies in recent years) by dismantling Navy 26-2. Savoldi romped to three TDs, carrying 11 times for 123 yards. Clarence Kaplan, fresh off the third string, ran for 96 yards on six carries, a good measure of the depth of this team. Savoldi scored on runs following laterals from Brill, for 23 yards and 55 yards. He scored from the 8, without benefit of a lateral, before coming out of the game. Kaplan took over here, his runs setting the stage for Fritz Staab's TD and the final score.

Carnegie Tech was next, recently a tough opponent for

One of Rockne's most respected coaching opponents—Carnegie Tech's Wally Steffen.

the Irish, but Rockne's players were ready this time. The Irish defense kept Carnegie Tech penned up in their own end of the field; the one time they managed to drive into Irish territory they managed a score, but ND put up three for a 21-6 final score. In the second quarter, Rockne pulled out all the stops on his new-fangled offense—spinners, laterals, reverses, passes, with Schwartz culminating the brilliant series with a 13-yard TD to Kosky. After the teams traded interceptions, Schwartz slipped in for a 2-yard TD. Carnegie Tech's Eyth broke loose on a 72-yard TD run, their one venture into ND territory, but Schwartz got it back with a 44-yard TD pass to Conley.

The Irish went east to play Pittsburgh. After Rockne had the Irish doing offensive pyrotechnics against Carnegie Tech, the Panthers expected more of the same. But Rockne decided to keep it simple, using a grueling ground game for a 35-19 win. Notre Dame scored all of its TDs in the first half, starting with their first play from scrimmage—Schwartz's 60-yard TD run. This was followed by 1-yard TD blasts by Mullins and Savoldi, then a long-range score … Savoldi from 42 yards out with an interception. Bucky O'Connor ticked off runs of 32 and 45 yards to set up Mike Koken's 5-yard TD tally. Pitt managed two scoring drives and got a third TD with a fumble recovery.

Rockne took the team back home to meet Indiana, and put together a game plan that left the Hoosiers gasping for air after 432 yards of Notre Dame rushing. Savoldi rumbled 33 yards for a TD, Schwartz dashed 26 yards for a second, Brill powered in from the Hoosier 9 after Schwartz returned a kickoff 79 yards, and then Brill ended the festivities with a 23-yard TD burst. The Hoosiers mounted only 76 yards on the ground in a dozen or so futile possessions.

Marty Brill transferred to Notre Dame from Penn, then led the Irish in a 60-20 rout over his former team.

In the late '20s, schedules were not made up ahead of time by a decade, as is the case today. Rockne must have scheduled Penn while mindful of the fact that Marty Brill had come to the Fighting Irish from Penn, a Quaker reject...quite a turnaround. Brill had plenty of motivation for this game and Rockne enjoyed pasting teams from the east. So, Brill scored a 65-yard TD on his first carry. While he was in the game with the starting unit, the Irish staked themselves to a 43-0 lead over the mild-mannered Quakers. Brill tacked on two more long TD runs; single TDs were registered by Carideo, Savoldi, Schwartz, Mullins, and O'Connor. Penn never gained a first down against the Irish starters. One wonders what kind of verbal exchange took place among the Penn coaching staff, after the 60-20 rout by Notre Dame, with the rocket scientist who had told Brill he wasn't good enough for Quaker football.

Rockne and the Irish lost Joe Savoldi to Notre Dame's strict student life guidelines, in this case the school's stringent rule against marriage. Savoldi not only violated that rule (secretly), he went one further and was in the process of getting a divorce. Maybe it was one of those things that could have been pulled off if he had filed his papers in Bemidji, but he had it done in South Bend, more or less under the nose of the press, who still almost managed to stifle the story. But things had tightened up at Notre Dame and in college football in general since the heady days of Gipp. There wasn't much Rockne could do in this case, although he probably gave it a try. He did give Savoldi some money to help him out for the interim (Savoldi went into pro football with the Bears...Walter Halas, brother of George Halas, had coached for Rockne from 1920 until 1923, perhaps a link Rockne could rely on). Savoldi also gave wrestling a fling, as it were.

Sans a talent such as Savoldi's, many teams would be tempted to take a nosedive. Perhaps aware of such a possibility, Rockne managed to pull a rabbit named Dan Hanley out of his bag of tricks. Right on cue, Hanley promptly stuck it to Drake with a 32-yard TD run. Drake put together an answering scoring drive, but Schwartz hauled the ensuing kickoff all the way to the Drake 13-yard line. After a couple of plays, Carideo faked a pass and handed off to Brill for a 3-yard TD run. Schwartz had a hand in the rest of the scoring—passing to set up a Mullins TD in the third quarter, then a 43-yard TD romp of his own to settle the score at 28-7.

It had been fairly smooth sailing for the Irish thus far in the season. Northwestern threatened the whole season with a great effort—reaching the Irish 5-yard line twice in the first half before the Irish defense stopped them. With ten minutes left in the game, the score stood at 0-0. Rockne must have been beside himself, but Schwartz took the edge off with an 18-yard TD scamper, followed shortly by Hanley's 1-yard score, to give ND a difficult 14-0 win.

Notre Dame met Army before 110,000 at Soldier Field (one wonders why it took this long for this pairing to have a game in this stadium). The Cadets entered the game undefeated, with only a tie to mar their season. It was a great game, especially if you like defense; terrible field conditions hampered both offenses. Nevertheless, Rockne's charges managed to pull off a "perfect play" that resulted in a 54-yard TD run by Schwartz. Army showed its mettle by blocking an Irish kick moments later, but an aroused Notre Dame team blocked the PAT try to preserve a 7-6 victory.

The season's finale would be against USC in LA. Rockne had lost the services of Mullins in the rough and tumble of the Army game. There was Hanley, of course, but Rockne knew that USC was spoiling for a fight— undefeated and winning by big margins each week. Savoldi was long gone, of course. So Rockne pulled off one of his all-time tricks (which would be impossible under today's strict rules): he had Bucky O'Connor, the second-string right halfback behind Brill, practice at fullback at the various pit stops on the long train ride to the west coast. But wait, he wasn't just working at fullback, he was dressed as Hanley (no matter that he was 5 inches shorter and 15 pounds lighter) and carefully instructed to look as bad as he could reasonably be expected to look—but especially slow and given to losing the handle on the ball at inopportune times. Francis Wallace was in the know (can anyone imagine a journalist today holding back on something like this?); the west coast reporters never learned the truth but kept spreading the intelligence about how slow and inept the Irish fullback was. In fact, O'Connor was almost as fast as had been the speedy Elder. In sum, USC would never know what hit them.

Before the game, Rockne tried a new motivational tactic—he had the team's trainer wrap his legs with the rubber sheathing then in use for victims of phlebitis. One wonders if there were any more tricks left for in Rockne's repertoire. On the field, the first thing that did hit USC was none other than O'Connor—on an 80-yard TD run in the second quarter. He also registered a 7-yard TD burst with a lateral, but lost a 60-yard TD run due to a penalty. For the game, Rockne's poor little fullback averaged 11 yards per carry. Other Irish scores came via a Trojan fumble that led to a 19-yard Schwartz TD pass to Carideo and a Hanley interception capped by a Nick Lukats TD run from the Trojan 11. The Trojans struggled for 140 yards of total offense compared to the 433 total yards the Irish compiled. When Lukats crossed the goalline to make the score 27-0 (which included a USC safety), no one could know that it was to be the last score of the Rockne era at Notre Dame.

The 1930 team managed to outgain its opponents by more than a 2:1 ratio. Notre Dame compiled 3,546 yards rushing and passing (3,109 and 437, respectively). Opponents manged to gain 961 yards on the ground and another 599 yards passing, for a total of 1,560 yards—almost 2,000 yards less than the Irish offense. It is

The first college team to repeat as an undefeated national champ—the 1930 starters.

important to note that Rockne's modern reputation has been intimately tied to the forward pass, but the 1930 results show a 7:1 dominance of running over passing. With their second consecutive undefeated season, Notre Dame officially became the first college to claim back-to-back undisputed national championships. The rejoicing was not very long or intense for, by now, the Depression had set in.

With the win over USC, Rockne's life work as Notre Dame's head coach was completed. He had won 105 games, lost 12, and tied 5 for the best winning percentage (.897) among coaches with more than ten years' experience. In the games he played in, or coached under Harper, and those in which he was the head coach, covering a period of twenty-one years, Rockne participated in 156 wins, 18 losses, and 9 ties, for a career winning percentage of .877 over 183 Notre Dame football games. For perspective consider that in more than 1,000 Notre Dame games, from 1887 to 1998, the Irish winning percentage is .759. Rockne's percentage as head coach is almost 20% better than the school's historical winning rate (which is the highest among major colleges). In his lifetime football experience under the Dome, Rockne's winning percentage is more than 15% higher than the school's overall record.

He coached one more game though—at the request of New York mayor Jimmy Walker, an all-star team of former Notre Dame stars played the New York Giants in a fund-raising effort for the unemployed. The former Irish players lost to the professionals, but as a gesture on behalf of the social good, it is fitting as Rockne's final effort. It also seems appropriate that Rockne's last

New York Mayor Jimmy Walker and Rockne, who responded to the Mayor's appeal for a charity exhibition game as the Depression menaced America.

stint on the sidelines finds him surrounded by his former stars, demonstrating the faith in sportsmanship he had been preaching on a regular basis throughout the period of the overemphasis issue.

After New Year's, Rockne went to the Mayo Clinic for a check up. It was a good news/bad news report—the phlebitis had improved but its threat would always be with him. He would not have to continue to follow the curtailed activity schedule of 1929 and 1930, but he could never again expect to be the physically active coach he had been in the past. He was really pleased to learn that he would not have to be confined to a wheelchair during spring practice.

From the Mayo Clinic, the Rockne family went to Coral Gables, Florida, where he had spent part of his convalescence the year before. Here he tried to relax and continue his recovery but nevertheless found himself talking football with his cronies. He was already beginning his plans for spring practice.

In late March, he left his family in Florida to return to Notre Dame and start spring drills. Rockne was looking forward to having Ed "Moose" Krause move up to the varsity, among other players. The coach was also planning a trip to the west coast to coincide with the start up of practice. Things were well organized for a good start in the spring, he found.

Above, The Rockne living room at the family home in South Bend, not far from the Notre Dame campus.

Below, Knute Rockne and his son Knute Rockne, Jr.

Rockne dropped in at his Studebaker office, sharing a few jokes and shaking hands with his friends there, including Paul Castner. He next went to Chicago to celebrate an early birthday for his mother. Part of the evening of March 30 was spent with his syndicate chief, Christy Walsh, a major figure in Rockne's various interests. Surely they spoke of the business trip to Los Angeles, one that involved a Lew Ayres movie.

From Chicago, Rockne took a train to Kansas City to visit a classmate, Dr. D. M. Nigro, and to see his boys, Bill and Knute, Jr., who attended the Pembroke School in Kansas City, having returned there from the Florida trip. Rockne waited at the train station to see his boys. They were late, so he called to check on his flight, perhaps it could be held a few minutes. He was able to wait a few minutes more but had to leave the train station and hurry to the airport. He missed seeing his boys by twenty minutes.

In spite of his hurrying to the airport, there were more delays there. For one, the weather was ominous,

Knute Rockne Jr.

threatening. One of the passengers took a moment to send a telegram to his family, announcing that he would be flying to California with the famous Knute Rockne. Eventually, however, Rockne and five other passengers boarded the Fokker Trimotor operated by TAT Transcontinental Western airline. A few minutes after boarding, the plane took off. Rockne settled into his seat, thankful that the plane was not filled with passengers. He propped up one of his bad legs, still wrapped in rubber, to give it some relief. The plane was scheduled to stop in Wichita to pick up more passengers and mail bags. After forty minutes in the air, the airport control room in Kansas City heard the anxious voice of one of the flight crew. He sought advice about the weather. The controller asked if he wanted to return to Kansas City. The voice replied, "I can't answer. We're too busy."

The voice may have been that of the plane's pilot, Robert Fry, who had once crash-landed a plane in China and then escaped from the marauding gangs that controlled the countryside. Fry could handle himself well in an emergency.

Rockne's plane never made it to Wichita. Over Bazaar, Kansas, not too far from Jesse Harper's big spread, off course, struggling in subfreezing temperatures, buffeted by a severe storm, the Fokker crashed in a field at 10:47 a.m. A local farmer, Ed Baker, recalled hearing the labored whine of the plane's big engines, then an explosion before seeing the big silver plane spilling its passengers from the fuselage in its death dive straight down

Examples of the grief
felt by the public following Rockne's
untimely death in 1931.

Example of the grief felt by the public following
Rockne's untimely death in 1931.

from an altitude of 650 feet. Part of the right wing flipped spasmodically through the air; sacks of mail streamed from the fuselage.

Several other local people knew that something was awry. The mail plane almost never flew over this part of the state. They heard the struggling engines and the crash, then they rushed to the scene. The plane had crashed almost perpendicular to the earth near the crest of a small hill. The tail assembly, the only relatively undamaged section of the aircraft, had crumpled forward over the crushed fuselage. There was no fire. There were no survivors.

A few feet to the right of the shattered fuselage lay a mangled body. The farmers immediately noticed that one leg of this crash victim was carefully wrapped in rubber.

Quickly realizing that there was nothing to be done to help possible survivors, onlookers started taking away bits and pieces from the crashed plane. When

Mourners overflowed the Sacred Heart church on the Notre Dame campus for Rock's funeral service.

crash investigators arrived at the scene later that day, more than half of the pertinent parts of the plane were missing. Eventually, a variety of possible causes for the crash were proposed: ice build-up tore off the wing, a structural flaw broke it off, the right propeller came off and severed the wing, maneuvering by the pilot stressed the wing beyond its limits, and so forth. The plane was not well designed for visual inspection of the wings, according to Paul Castner.

The Golden Age of American sports now had its first famous idol to reach the status of martyr.

Not surprisingly, Rockne's death led to an outpouring of public grief seldom experienced short of the deaths of presidents. CBS put together the first nationwide radio broadcast of the funeral proceedings that took up much of Easter week, 1931. Hundreds of condolence telegrams flooded the University. People wrote grief-stricken poetry that appeared in local newspapers and editorial columns. Other newspapers featured editorial cartoons that attempted to convey the public's sense of loss and appreciation of Rockne's achievements. The Studebaker Corporation marketed its Rockne Six heavily for two years after his death. King Haakon of Norway honored Rockne with a posthumous knighthood. The efforts to memorialize Rockne with a building in his honor at Notre Dame began almost at once. Delayed by the ravages of the Depression, the building had its cornerstone laid in 1938; it was completed and dedicated in 1939. To this day, the Rockne Memorial building sits prominently at one end of the main academic quad, opposite the O'Shaughnessey Hall of Liberal Arts. "The Rock" is not located near the impressive grouping of structures devoted to athletics today at Notre Dame, which are clustered near the football stadium that Rockne helped will into existence. It is as if, however, his presence embraces much of the campus and is not isolated merely to athletics.

THIS IS AS IT SHOULD BE.

Irish players huddle at their coach's grave as the funeral service concludes.

Outside Sacred Heart church on the Notre Dame campus
for Rock's funeral service.

Laying and dedication of cornerstone in 1938.

Mrs. Rockne at her husband's memorial dedication in 1939.

Hunk Anderson's pensive moment at the 1939 dedication of the Rockne Memorial (left).

Knute Rockne Memorial construction,
early stages (above) and middle stages (below).

The finished version of the Knute Rockne Memorial (left).

Interior shot of the Knute Rockne Memorial dedicated in 1938 (above).

Archway to the entrace of the
Knute Rockne Memorial (below).

The front entrance to the Rockne Memorial (above and right).

INTERVIEWS

The following four interviews were held during the last weeks of 1979 when I was in South Bend for

research at Notre Dame's International Sports and Games Collection regarding this book. The people inter-

viewed all had had a direct connection to Knute Rockne. In most cases, the person being interviewed has a very

clear memory of Rockne. In some cases, those being interviewed do not remember the details with total accuracy;

after all, fifty years or more had passed at the time. All of these men have since passed on. Their thoughts thus

constitute a precious legacy regarding Knute Rockne. May God bless them, one and all.

INTERVIEW WITH PROFESSOR RICHARD SULLIVAN:

Richard Sullivan was for many years a professor of English at Notre Dame. He was one of my English professors during my undergraduate years; I also served as his student assistant for his creative writing courses for two years. Professor Sullivan and I had been friends for many years, and I recalled that when he was teaching Mr. Sullivan often referred to his experiences as an undergraduate at Notre Dame in the Twenties. This fact remained with me, and, when the opportunity came for my work in the Sports and Games Research Collection, the decision to interview Mr. Sullivan was an obvious one.

Professor Richard Sullivan

After graduation from Notre Dame in 1930, Prof. Sullivan spent some time in Europe, especially Paris, where he came to know many of the writers who made that city a special place in the Thirties. Later, he returned to spend a career teaching at Notre Dame. He has been in a position to see Rockne's influence first-hand as a fledgling player and as a student and then to observe the growth of the university during his teaching career. He admitted to coming to Notre Dame with the high hopes of winning a place on the varsity football team. He did, in fact, try out for the freshman team as a 145-pound halfback, but found himself overmatched early in his effort as he attempted to return a punt but was obliterated by a varsity player, 220-pound tackle Joe Boland (later the voice of the Irish on radio broadcasts). This ignominious treatment disabused Sullivan forever of his youthful plans to make the varsity under Rockne. In spite of his abrupt departure from the game, he counted for years among his closest friends former Irish quarterback Chet Grant, who maintained a very close relationship to Notre Dame football over seven decades.

The interview was held at Professor Sullivan's home not far from the Notre Dame campus. It overlooked the St. Joseph River and was filled with the memorabilia and paraphernalia of a life spent writing, reading, and teaching. Sullivan was a small man, then in somewhat frail health, but nevertheless with a characteristic twinkle in his eye and an omnipresent pipe. This interview was held on December 16, 1979.

STEELE: You apparently came to Notre Dame in the fall of 1926 after having been a high school quarterback. You had heard of Rockne before then?

SULLIVAN: Oh yes.

STEELE: What kind of impression did you have of him before you ever got to the campus?

SULLIVAN: Oh, I don't know. He was a great name, a different kind of name than Red Grange, but Red Grange was big at that time, you know. [Rockne] was just a big name in football. I wouldn't say he was the reason I came to Notre Dame, though I did want to play football. And I knew he was awfully good. But I came to Notre Dame I think for many other reasons, most of which probably were more important than that. But certainly he was known, and I should say that every high school kid playing football at that time knew Rockne …

Red Grange and Bob Zuppke

STEELE: Now, more specifically, did he represent some sort of masculine role model for you or anything like that at all?

SULLIVAN: Of course at that time I would have never thought in those terms and I don't think he did. Using the term as it's used now, I don't think so, no.

STEELE: You have said that you had the impression that Rockne was very personable when you would meet him on campus.

SULLIVAN: *Very* personable. I don't mean that he stopped you and slapped your back. But he was a gracious personality. If a freshman walked across the campus at Notre Dame and met Rockne, the freshman's alone and Rockne's alone, Rockne would say "Hello, kid," or "Hello, boy," or "Hello, fella" and in a kind of gruff voice, you know, but very friendly. And the kid would feel kind of honored that this guy had talked to him.

STEELE: What do you think, then, was Rockne's most significant personal characteristic?

SULLIVAN: . . . . Well, he had a kind of rather brusque, rough charm. He was an attractive personality. And his reputation, I suppose, enhanced that whole thing of his being an attractive personality. … my own direct impression as far as I can remember was one of his being a person of great charm, great attractiveness. As a person, he was a kind of man you thought, "I can talk to this man. And he'll talk to me. And he'll listen."

STEELE: So, charisma, perhaps.

SULLIVAN: Yes.

STEELE: How much of the myth surrounding Rockne was due to Rockne's own self-dramatization? He apparently had a capacity for creating himself. . . .

SULLIVAN: Yes.

STEELE: and was very aware of the process and what not.

SULLIVAN: Yes, I think he was a—and I mean this in a flattering way—he was a great operator. He could handle situations in a way that generally would make himself, his teams, Notre Dame, look good. And as to all this myth, there is a Rockne myth, certainly. I don't know how to separate the myths from Rockne with any precision. But I think that he contributed somewhat to his own myth. I don't think he thought of it in terms of a Rockne myth. He just thought it was good, maybe he used the word "publicity," good public relations. He certainly was not one to miss a chance at improved public relations.

STEELE: But this was not in a self-serving way?

SULLIVAN: Oh, not a bit, no. I've never had the impression that Rockne was in any sense a self-serving man. And I'm happy that he wasn't. If you're a self-server, there's something a little suspicious. But, no, he was, I think, a much more complicated and deep man than he gave the impression of being. But I think he was a generous [man] and, when you use the word "good' you really mean something. He was a good man, I think.

STEELE: But he also enjoyed his success.

SULLIVAN: Oh, I'm *sure* he did. He delighted in it.

STEELE: [Journalist] Westbrook Pegler apparently really bothered him by pinning him in one case. He hurt him by calling him an "oil can," at one point, that "poured champagne."

SULLIVAN (a bit incredulous): An oil can that poured champagne.

STEELE: Yes, he said he was a battered up oil can that poured champagne. (Sullivan chuckles.) Which is, as a matter of fact, something that's kind of dogged Rockne. Pegler has his own myth; he's a good writer and all that. Apparently Pegler thought that Rockne really did like the success, and maybe even the financial success. You know he was quite big in Studebaker at the time of his death. He even had a car named for him for a while which fell through with the Depression.

(Sullivan mulls this over while he lights his pipe).

STEELE: Just a personal opinion now; this is a hard one—do you think that there's any possibility that Gipp, talking to Rock in 1920, actually made a death-bed request? We know for a fact what Rockne said to his players for the 1928 Army game. Then Chevigny said, "That's one for the Gipper" when he scored his touchdown in the second half. That much we know happened. There were people who heard Rockne say all this to the team, and the players from Army and Notre Dame heard Chevigny say that as he crossed the goal line. Now, what's your estimation? Do you think that Gipp actually said this to Rockne? Number one, do you think it's possible or number two, does it even matter?

SULLIVAN: Number one, it is possible. (Pause.) Number two, yes, perhaps in the interest of truth, it does matter. Certainly, I would never be able to pronounce on it, whether it happened or not.

STEELE: You take it as truth?

SULLIVAN: No, I don't take it as truth. I say I think it matters whether it's the truth or not. I'd like to know myself whether it's true or not. (Laughs.)

STEELE: I'll tell you if I ever find out.

SULLIVAN: But I think, Mike, honestly, that I find it quite compatible with my own image of Rockne that he would make it up. Though I don't mean for a moment that it isn't quite possible that Gipp did say that to Rockne on his death bed. It could be. Or Gipp could have said something close to that and Rockne could have elaborated a little.

STEELE: Sure, and of course, in the throes of death as Gipp was for two or three days; he was in the hospital for fourteen days or more. Of course, if it were a mere fabrication, Rockne would not have been aware of any moral issue.

SULLIVAN: Not a bit, no.

STEELE: Taking a death-bed . . . .

SULLIVAN: I think he used it, I'm sure he used it, in terms of the standard pep talk, you know. Lord, we've all had pep talks in one way or another, and they don't always adhere strictly to the very literal truth. So I don't think Rockne was thinking of this as a lie. Indeed, he might not have thought about it two minutes before he said it.

STEELE: Well, there's evidence—Grantland Rice had Rockne in his apartment the night before the game. Rice lived in the upper Fifties, some nice place in New York. The game...was played in Yankee Stadium. Rockne said to Rice, "You know, I'm worried about this game and might have to use George Gipp to win it." (Pause) [On another matter,] what do you think was the degree to which Rockne was

Sartorial splendor
and Rockne.

responsible for the present close relationship between excellence in academics and athletics here at Notre Dame? He would have stressed that, don't you think?

SULLIVAN: I don't know. Well, yes, I think if you'd asked Rockne about it he would certainly stress the academic too, but whether he had any connection between this sort of program of excellence, particularly in academic affairs, whether he did anything to start that, I don't know. I trace that more to Hesburgh [the president of Notre Dame at the time of the interview]. Or perhaps I should qualify that. Father Cavanaugh, before Hesburgh, started the general idea. And Father Moore, Father Phillip S. Moore, who was I think very much neglected in the community, was at various times secretary of the Graduate School, dean of the Graduate School, then he became vice-president of academic affairs, but he was always pushing the idea of excellence, excellence, excellence.

STEELE: What was the time frame on that for Father Moore?

SULLIVAN: Moore came back here in about 1935 or 1936, from three years in Paris, after doing his doctoral work at Catholic University. He died, it seems to me, about 1970 or 1971. I may be a little prejudiced in favor of him because he was a very dear friend of mine, of ours, but I don't think that my personal bias would make me feel that he was important if he wasn't. He was behind these two presidents that I've mentioned. I don't see the connection with Rockne and the general drive toward excellence in academic affairs as a public thing. But, Mike, look, when I was a student here in the late Twenties, I think we were awfully good academically. We had a terrible number of soft spots—dead wood. But I had teachers at that time that I'll never forget. They were great. I had some that were very poor, but I think if you go to any school today, you'll find on any faculty some dead wood, soft spots. [Sullivan's career at Notre Dame, from the 1930s to the 1970s, spanned a period in which the ramifications of the role and impact of football at Notre Dame became a controversial issue among faculty members. Note his reluctance here to see Rockne as central in any way to the University's current academic profile. For many faculty at the school, the prominent status of football is regrettable. One wonders how many times in his long career that Professor Sullivan had to mull over this issue].

STEELE: Has the role of football on the college campus changed much since the 1920-1930 era? Does it have about the same impact as an event?

SULLIVAN: I guess in general about the same, I would think. You see, in the late Twenties, when I was an undergraduate, Notre Dame was, I think, around three thousand; maybe it wasn't quite that. And it was a much cozier, close-in atmosphere than there is today. And football I don't think had the national importance that it has today.

STEELE: Probably because of the media?

SULLIVAN: Yes, there was no television. As an undergraduate, did you ever hear of the Grid-o-gram?

STEELE: Yes, right.

SULLIVAN: In the old gym, you paid a quarter to get in.

STEELE: **And you could watch a light move . . . .**

SULLIVAN: Right, watch a light move. And that light was Chevigny, the halfback or something, you know.

STEELE: **In the 1920 Indiana game, this was very important. Notre Dame was getting the socks beat off, and the students watched that light move up the field. It was coming back for a win, ultimately. Yes, I've read about that. Now, obviously it wasn't part of my experience [in the sixties].**

SULLIVAN: That was the way we watched all games away from the campus. The old Cartier Field was just only open bleachers. It was a horrible way to watch a football game.

STEELE: **It had only about fifteen thousand capacity.**

SULLIVAN: Something like that. Of course, it had no restrooms in Cartier Field. But how different that would be from the stadium today. And ours isn't one of the big, big whopping stadiums.

STEELE: **It's just a medium-sized stadium. [The recent expansion changed this].**

SULLIVAN: And also pro football was just really beginning. It had begun maybe ten years before, but it wasn't anything important.

STEELE: **Rockne was against it. He played in a few games, to help make ends meet, and he also played against Jim Thorpe.**

SULLIVAN: I didn't know that.

STEELE: **But just a couple of games and then he quit. He was against it because he thought that after your playing days were over you should go into coaching or teaching or business or something.**

SULLIVAN: I think he was right. We've built up a kind of phony profession for athletes for about ten years of their lives after school.

STEELE: **Yes. Then they're often stuck after that. Now, just**

Jim Thorpe

personal observation, perhaps knowledge—to what extent did Rockne run the games from the sidelines? Did his quarterbacks have quite a bit of freedom? I know that the substitution rules were much more rigorous.

SULLIVAN: I think they had so much freedom by comparison with most teams today when each play is sent in. They were almost totally free; the quarterback called the game, except when a substitute came in. And once in a while a substitute would be sent in deliberately to put in a play. But that would happen once a game. Because once that substitute was in he had to stay that quarter or somebody else had to come in for him. I don't remember the details of the rules, but if you went out in a given quarter, you couldn't come back until the next quarter or the next half—I don't remember.

STEELE: Not only that, they had a stipulation that you couldn't say anything to the quarterback for the first play.

SULLIVAN: That was true, yes.

STEELE: But Rockne had his man named Johnny "One-Play" O'Brien who was only good for the long pass, and that's reportedly the only thing O'Brien could do. They sent him in and everyone knew what the play was supposed to be, but he would never say what it was for the first play because it was illegal.

SULLIVAN: Yes.

STEELE: Now this last question. Again, Grantland Rice, one time supposedly took Rockne to a party in New York and there was the East Coast's most famous magician. This guy was doing tricks with Rockne, and he was so fast that Rockne couldn't follow him, even when he was using Rockne's own hands. It was a trick using footballs; he would place a ball in one hand and a ball in the other; he'd do something and then there would be two balls in one hand and none in the other. Rockne never could figure the trick out, and I can't either. But he was so taken by this that he decided to start sending his quarterbacks to magicians. *(Chuckles.)* Do you have any information that he ever did that? Did you ever hear any rumors about it?

SULLIVAN: Never heard of that in my life before, Mike.

STEELE: Grantland Rice claims that this happened. He didn't say that he actually ended up doing it, but that he would have liked to try it.

SULLIVAN: Now if we take Grantland Rice as telling the truth here, and let's do that, it could have been that Rockne said something in a flip moment like, "Boy, I ought to send my quarterbacks to you." But, you see, the quarterback in Rockne's day didn't handle the ball any more than any of the other backs. He was the signal caller by tradition always. But he was also a backfield man. He didn't squat behind the center. He might sometimes go side-saddle [that is, move right or left from center with the shift]. But most of the time he was lined up as a blocker, after he had called the signal. And occasionally, if he was a runner, he could run. But he was always an up back rather than a tailback.

STEELE: Well, Rockne was captivated by the deception. So much of Rockne's system was based on deception anyway.

SULLIVAN: Yes, but he didn't have the quarterback deception that we have today because, see, it wasn't until Leahy came that we put in the T.

STEELE: And that's where you get the ball shoveled into the runner and pulled back out for the fake.

SULLIVAN: The nearest thing to that in the Rockne teams that I remember—I don't remember the name of the play— but it was a direct pass [snap] to the fullback from the center. The fullback was playing back perhaps three and a half to four yards. And the halfbacks would be on both sides of him; it was really a T-formation. But the fullback then got the ball direct, and he could run with the other backs cutting in front of him or he could pivot this way (demonstrates) and hand the ball off to a halfback that way or a halfback this way or he could complete the pivot and go straight through, which made it a kind of draw.

STEELE: Thank you! You've just told me what a spinner play is. That's what Rockne called a spinner play.

SULLIVAN: Yes.

STEELE: That actually developed into what's now called the Delaware Veer, which Theismann and Tom Clements used here.

SULLIVAN: Explain the Delaware Veer.

STEELE: Well, the Delaware Veer has the quarterback up under center, and your backs split behind him, with perhaps a flanker out wide, or the backs are even stacked in an I; all the quarterback does is take the snap, turn around, take a step or two and the backs can cross for a hand-off, or one of them can be in motion as the quarterback gets the ball, who can shovel it right or left, he can keep, they can smash into the

Frank Leahy, one of Rockne's best
students of football

line, or they can become pass receivers. It's very effective due to the deception that can occur, except instead of using the fullback as the pivotal man, it uses the quarterback. Now, talking about the shift, you have said that one of the amazing things to you was watching it and the linemen in their shift. You said that it was almost like watching something musical, as if it had a beat to it.

SULLIVAN: It had not so much—well, a beat if you like, yes, it was done as if to music, to the beat of music, and the entire [backfield] would be rocking.

STEELE: Rhythm perhaps would be a better word.

SULLIVAN: Rhythm might be better, yes. But it was done to an absolute cadence. I can't understand how they ever ... they must have taken hours of practice ... When you'd see eleven men out there rocking to this beautiful cadence [Sullivan recalls the shift involving all eleven players; I have been unable to verify this beyond the backfield, unless there was a slight surge just before the snap], it had something of the effect of ballet. It was beautiful. And, at a certain moment, when they were rocking, let's say the line and backfield are both rocking right, just at the instant when they reached extreme movement to the right, just three inches say, the ball is snapped. Suppose they go right. The other team is perhaps standing upright; they aren't rocking. Everybody on the Notre Dame team, eleven men, are moving to the right just at the instant the ball is snapped. Think of the advantage that gives them in the thrust to the right. Now the next time the line may rock right and the backfield may be at the extreme left of the rock as the ball is snapped. They could have weak-side play with a lot of effect for the backfield, and the line is just recovering from its right side and going left as the play is developed. Instantaneous. Beautiful.

STEELE: You said something very interesting there because you used the word "ballet." This is important because I keep seeing dancing references and artistic references in the books. And it turns out that when the one-second rule was passed against the shift, that you had to be set for a second, Rockne got his backs to count to a *second point two*! That's how close he timed it. They would practice this into the fourth game of the season with a count; they would actually have a cadence. Then, after the fourth game, they had internalized it so they didn't have to use the actual count. But they knew what a second point two was from a second point four. That's incredible.

SULLIVAN: Oh, it is.

STEELE: Notice that he was doing all this without the benefit of film. That's one reason why his scouting system was so big. It's another reason why he used the so-called shock troops. If he had lived into the period when there was widespread dissemination of films, he would have pitched a couple of these things because he could have just used the films to detect weaknesses.

INTERVIEW WITH ED "MOOSE" KRAUSE

The interview with Moose Krause, the long-time Athletic Director at Notre Dame, was held on December 17, 1979. Krause entered Notre Dame as a freshman in the fall of the year that Richard Sullivan had graduated, 1930. He played freshman football and basketball while Rockne was still alive and also some of the spring practice before Rockne's accidental death in Kansas. At 6 feet, 4 inches and 235 pounds, he was a living testament to Rockne's plans to move toward ever larger teams because the shift was relatively crippled compared to its heyday in the mid-Twenties.

An excellent athlete, Krause became Notre Dame's first two-sport All-American. He later coached basketball in the 1940s and football at two other colleges before returning to spend the rest of his career under the Dome. He became Athletic Director in 1949, three years before Father Theodore Hesburgh became

Ed "Moose" Krause

president of the university. These two, along with the later addition of Father Edmund Joyce, have supervised the continued excellence of Notre Dame's athletic traditions—emphasizing a balance of academics with athletics, a notable absence of an athletes' residence system, an elaborate intramural athletic system, and the highest of ethical standards for Notre Dame coaches and athletes.

The interview was held in Krause's spacious but crowded office in the Joyce Athletic and Convocation Center, just across the street from the football stadium the construction of which had been supervised by Rockne. The walls were covered with mementos of past Irish luminaries and teams. High above his large desk was proudly displayed a set of Texas longhorns—obviously the result of the 1978 Cotton Bowl victory over Texas. Krause was an impressive physical specimen even in his sixties. He seemed comfortable with his bulk draped in a large swivel chair. As the interview got under way, he punctuated his remarks with gestures dominated by a big cigar—the same trait Rockne had.

It was my great honor to work again with Moose over the years after this interview. He helped considerably with my *Fighting Irish Football Encyclopedia* and served as a co-signer at one of my book signings two weeks before his death in 1992. God bless, Moose.

STEELE: I have first a couple of personal questions for you. What were your feelings immediately upon hearing of Rockne's death?

KRAUSE: Well, I'd say I felt I had lost a person who was very close to me. When I say close, there were three hundred freshmen out for the Notre Dame freshman's team when I was a freshman in 1930. But I would say that Rockne knew most of them, I felt, very personally. I recall an incident when my dad arrived here after I had been here for three months, and he came over to visit with my brother Phil and me. We were both freshmen at the time. We had lunch at the cafeteria. On the way out, why, he said he'd like to meet Knute Rockne, the coach, after all he'd heard about him. I said to my dad, "He's so busy. Maybe we'll stop by and see him." I was trying to duck my father on that because I knew how busy Rockne was. On the other hand, as we were walking out of the cafeteria, he was headed for the caf [cafeteria] right in our direction. My dad said, "There he is. Can I meet him now?"

Just then Coach Rockne came right directly to where my brother Phil and I were standing there with my dad. He went right directly to us and said, "Moose and Phil, how are you doing in your studies?" That was the first question he asked us. Naturally, I had the opportunity of introducing the famous coach to my dad. That he recognized us was something that we appreciated, naturally. But he had the same feeling with the other players too on the team. He knew the players by their names; he had a fabulous memory for names. And also he was deeply concerned, number one, which we are today here at Notre Dame and follow his philosophy—he was always concerned with the academic progress of every student he had under his wing as a coach. And this was the greatest thing that I remember about him at that time.

Now you mentioned a question about my feelings when he died. I was in Chicago at the time; that's where we lived. When we heard about Rockne dying, naturally both of us just cried like kids because we had lost our father. He was that close to us even though we had only known him a short time. That was from September until—well, we met him that spring [1930] before—but until March 1931, when he was killed in the airplane. So we thought we had lost someone that was close to us even though we knew him for a short time. People wonder how you can get close to a person in that short of a time. Well, we had the experience of being under his wing in a sense. We were [playing] on the freshmen team in the fall of 1930, when we had the undefeated [varsity] team. We had an opportunity to scrimmage against the [varsity] and get involved with Rockne in a sense and see his great psychological effect on all of us even though we were freshmen and not even able to play in the games. Naturally, freshmen in those days weren't eligible. But we felt a closeness to Rockne. It was an amazing thing because those three hundred freshmen felt they were a part of Rockne's team in a sense. And he also had about three hundred boys out for varsity. Now that's six hundred boys out for football [out of a student body of perhaps less than three thousand]. And with a coaching staff of only four on the varsity and about four on the freshman team you wonder how he was able to maneuver that many people around, control that many people. He had an amazing faculty for inspiring people, getting them to feel close, to be a part. In fact, my ambition was as a freshman hoping some day to be on the second team! Never feeling that I'd ever make the first team. Just to be on Rockne's squad was a great compliment. As an example, in our freshman year, we didn't have as many scholarships as today. My brother Phil and I [each] happened to get one—which were working scholarships in those days. We had to hash and wait on tables in the dining room. And we were fortunate to get that. But there were only a few of those. Most of the kids who came, I can remember, there were probably a hundred on our freshman team who were captains and all-state players from all over the country who came here to be under the wing, the tutelage of Knute Rockne. He had a great image that no other coach even to this day has ever had. Boys from around the country wanted to play for Rockne. This was the feeling we had as players ourselves. But when he died we felt like we had not only lost a great coach but a friend, a person who was like a father, as I mentioned earlier.

Pat O'Brien at Knute
Rockne's grave.

STEELE: You've already answered three or four of my other questions. What, then, did Rockne come to mean to you as you've molded your career in athletics here since 1949? Obviously, you've interacted with him as a man and with his influence on the univerity and what the university stands for. You've already mentioned that he is in several ways still living for some who haven't even met him. Obviously, perhaps even the people who might read this book.

KRAUSE: You can imagine. Here, I've only known him as a freshman for a limited number of months. You can understand my feelings. But just imagine the players who were under his wings for *four* years. They have as strong a feeling as I do or perhaps even stronger. In fact, my whole life, I think, I've followed the philosophy of Knute Rockne. As an example, he used to talk to the team; he had meetings every noon, incidentally, even when we were freshmen. You wonder how I got to know Coach Rockne; well, he had meetings every spring at noontime and every fall. And during the fall of 1930 we had the opportunity of going to all of the meetings that he had in the spring until his death.

Moose with championship ring.

STEELE: This was like a football clinic that he ran.

KRAUSE: Yes, every minute was exciting from the point of view that he had something important to tell us about. Not only about football, but a way of life in a sense. And that football will play a part in our lives but that our academics would play as much a part. He had a great ability to mold us to a point of view of learning the values of a college education more so than even competition in athletics. But, as far as my life is concerned, I've tried to pattern my philosophy with Knute Rockne's. I just talked to a newspaperman in New York just a moment ago, talking to him about our schedule, what kind of a season we had this year, what was my impression of the season. I told him we won seven games and lost four. But in those four games we lost to four good teams. I pointed out that we had the toughest schedule in the country. So this was Rockne's philosophy: We want to play the best. And if we win we gain prestige. But if we lose there's no disgrace in losing to a good football team. Consequently, when I concluded my conversation with the newspaperman, he realized that seven and four is not a bad season. It wasn't a successful season from the point of view of Notre Dame because our alumni expect us to win all the games. But, on the other hand, there are hundreds of schools that would like a seven and four season. But anyway, the lessons I've learned from Rockne, he talked about in these meetings we had in the fall and spring about the value of competition. And he used athletics and football as a point that would be a great development in our lifetime from the point of view of teamwork, cooperation, being able to accept adversity, how to win properly, self-discipline, loyalty. [Krause's list of benefits should be compared with a similar list offered later by Paul Castner in his interview.] He talked about all these things. And I think in my case I tried to follow that pattern all through my life as a coach at St. Mary's College, Holy Cross, here at Notre Dame. And now as athletic director I still follow his philosophy. We want to play the best. We feel we talk to our squad just like Rockne does. Al of our freshmen come in here, and we visit with them before the season starts. We tell them the most important thing to have as an objective at Notre Dame is to get a good, solid education, which we'll promise you. And on the other hand, you'll have an opportunity to play with a team that will be nationally favored; we'll be playing the top teams in the country. You'll have an opportunity to play football. It won't be the most important part of your education but certainly a good part that will develop you to become competitive in life, and life is a great big battle. These are the things that I learned from Rockne, and I've followed that all through my lifetime.

STEELE: In a word, what do you think was his most significant personal characteristic? You've referred to him as a father figure; you've followed his philosophy. But in his person-to-person relationship, even the time that he walked up to meet your dad, I know the man was very charismatic—there was charisma about him. What do you think it was?

KRAUSE: I think it was something that you felt that he had a personal interest in your life. You got the feeling that he was interested as much in what you did off the field as on the field. He spoke many times at his meetings I mentioned earlier of the value of living a proper life off-campus and being a representative of Notre Dame. Yes, I think the greatest thing I know about him personally was the fact that I felt that *he* knew *me* as a young man trying to get a good education, trying to play on the football team. I thought he had a personal interest in me. He was able to do that with all the boys on the team. That's why I think, even to this day, the boys who had an opportunity to play for him, or were in the same situation as I was, where you had *some* contact with this man, you'll always remember him as someone who had an interest in you and wanted to develop you as a full man. He talked about things I explained about today, about the education we want you to get at Notre Dame comprised of three areas— one is the intellectual, the spiritual, and the physical. Yes, he talked about the spiritual life of a human being or of players on the team. Protestants or Catholics, it didn't make any difference. He himself as you know was a convert. He had a great interest and felt that every boy should have a spiritual aim in his lifetime. So, those were some of the feelings I had about him.

STEELE: Very good. What do you think has been his major impact on the game as we know it?

KRAUSE: Some of the things that I see today Rockne was using those types of tactics or systems. As an example, the Rules Committee changed the rules twice because of the Rockne shift, the Notre Dame shift. But he conquered that by shifting and then stopping for a second. And then later on, I recall this very clearly, I remember a play book I still have today, that he gave us the winter before he was killed. And in there he had what he called spinner plays, what they call today misdirection plays. Well, Rockne had those plays in 1929 or 1930. These are the plays I see now in college football, and I see it in professional football. Of course, professional football now and college football is at its peak. I think we have the best game we've ever had.

STEELE: Don't you think we see, for instance, the shift's influence in the Dallas Cowboys offense? Isn't it an outgrowth of Rockne's use of deception?

KRAUSE: Yes, I have seen it in Dallas's offense; I also saw it in the Washington Redskins' offense yesterday when they shifted from the T-formation into a box. His philosophy of football, let me tell you something, his philosophy of football was interesting. The old-timers will tell you the same thing. I can still remember him saying, "If you can't run through them, then go around them. If you can't go around them, you go over them." It's a very simple formula. You saw the Dallas game yesterday. They went over them. They couldn't go through them to win

Jock Sutherland

the game. Sometimes our offense this year, we were trying to go through them all the time. I'd tell the coach, go over them when you can't run at them. That was Rockne's philosophy—if you can't run through them, go over them or around them.

STEELE: Well, he was very good at adjusting to the rules as they kept trying to pin him down on the shift. Apparently you yourself are a good example that he was moving toward a bigger team, because all of his success with the Four Horsemen and what not had been based on smaller backs and [increased overall] team speed.

KRAUSE: All right, but still the philosophy today in pro and college football, I've got to use both, is the same philosophy he had. He was the only coach of his time, the only coach. You've heard of Warner, and Alonzo Stagg, and [Bob] Zuppke and [Jock] Sutherland—they all were two-timing people [double-teaming]. Two blocks on one defensive man. In my time even, at about the top of his career, he then had single blocking, one man on one man. It's exactly what the pros are using today. Very seldom do they use two on one. They only do that maybe on passes. But on running plays they use what they call screen blocking. This is exactly what Rockne was doing with his quick-opening, fast backs, smaller backs, and small linemen. So, it's the same pattern today that these coaches now are using that he was using in the twenties, using the type of blocking they're using today. In all the blocking in those days was to put two guys on the end and two guys on the tackles. I know I was blocked by two guys all the time that I played [1931-1933]. But nowadays you watch these offenses by both pros and colleges—there's one guy blocking on one. All they have to do is screen and get the timing. Rockne was great for timing.

STEELE: Yes. When they put the one-second rule in he had those guys coached to know what a second point two was so they wouldn't be caught on the rules. Did he run with his backfields in slow motion for movements on particular cuts and patterns and what not? He actually claimed that he ran them in slow motion during his early practices, place the men step-by-step, even on his spinner plays.

KRAUSE: We did that. I think he would do that at times to make sure the timing was right from the point of view of telling the boys what direction they were going to. As an example, an off-tackle play, the right halfback had to block the tackle or the end, or the halfback would fake the block and go around and the fullback would block him. So he did have that.

STEELE: Stuhldreher in his book said that Rockne got part of his idea for the shift from watching a chorus line when they were in New York for one of their games. They went out for an evening and saw the Rockettes or something similar. I know that Harper used the shift in a fairly rudimentary fashion in 1915 or 1916. Then Rockne specialized by making the ends all the more important. I understand that the shift also involved the linemen. We no longer see this with the exception of an end who will move. You, as a tackle, would have been involved in the shift?

KRAUSE: Not as much as the end. You should check with Chet Grant. One of Rockne's great sayings was that football was not a game of muscle and brawn. It is a game of wit and intelligence.

STEELE: He himself had to do this given the body he was born with.

KRAUSE: That's right. Look at the Four Horsemen. Those little bitty guys. They were quick and had angles on these blockers.

STEELE: You knew Joe Savoldi. All my background reading indicates that Rockne was moving toward bigger backs as the shift was gradually encumbered with rules.

KRAUSE; I would say if he was alive he'd still be putting innovations in there. He'd probably be doing some of the things that some of the coaches are doing now. He'd have a big fullback to keep the defensive line steady by faking into the line like they do today. He did that with his spinner series, with the halfback spinning off the Notre Dame box, faking to the fullback, going into the line, he'd give to the halfback or get himself into the other direction. Misdirection plays we call them today. He had misdirection plays then.

STEELE: I thought that Parseghian's veer offense was real close to that.

KRAUSE: His misdirection plays were every close to Rockne's. Getting them off balance. That's what Rockne was great on. You see, Rockne, as far as his plays were concerned, had a simple offense. But the point was that he always had someone faking into the line who could have the ball. It was like the wishbone offense, where they fake to one and give it to another. They might give it to the first guy, they might give it to the second guy, or the third guy.

STEELE: To make the defense commit itself.

KRAUSE: Why, sure, he had all that stuff. You talk about the T-formation. Rockne had the T-formation even then *with* the Notre Dame box. He ran plays off the T-formation which is one of the offenses used by many teams today—running off the T-formation.

STEELE: One of the last things in his career was that he actually anticipated television.

KRAUSE: I was on the first television committee with the NCAA. It was a big concern about television hurting

Rockne and Carideo accepting
the Erskine Award
for the '30 national title.

college football. Now you get reams of publicity from the NCAA saying how football has better attendance and so on. And they claim that it's because of the curtailment of the plan. That's a lot of baloney. It's not because of the curtailment of the plan; it's the fact that people are getting to see good college football on television. Now you go back to the era of the Twenties when Rockne got on radio. As I said to the television people then, there was a big concern that Rockne with his radio broadcast of Notre Dame games was going to harm the smaller schools and other schools because then he would be captivating the public and have better recruiting and so on because he's on the radio. Well, it didn't harm football. I think radio helped football develop a lot because a lot of the games got on radio. Now it's the same thing with television. So I know in his mind he'd have been way ahead in television. We were, at Notre Dame incidentally, the first school to televise with any consistency in football. If we were allowed to do what we had planned, we could have had all of our games on national television, like we do with basketball and on radio with Mutual Broadcasting. [This came to pass in the Holtz era, with a contract for all home games with NBC; away games are also often televised]. This is something he dreamed about. We never had national or international broadcasting when he was here but we do now. But I think we try to follow Rockne's thinking there. He was always looking ahead. Notre Dame's got the greatest public relations value from international broadcasting and Mutual Broadcasting [world-wide radio broadcasts of Irish games]. It goes all over the world. Japan, as an example, they know all about Notre Dame. They've wanted us there for years. [The Irish had played Miami in Tokyo just three weeks before this interview].

STEELE: I heard the Cotton Bowl game when I was living in Tokyo in 1971.

KRAUSE: Yes. There he could see the value of the thing as we see it today. He knew that being on radio was going to help stimulate more interest, not only for Notre Dame but for all of college football. In 1928 he saved college football before the Carnegie Foundation. And then before that it was Theodore Roosevelt. Today it was Father Joyce, Edmund P. Joyce, our vice-president, who saved college football in the last four years when the

NCAA was going in for the needy clause where there would be more under the table and bad recruiting. He stopped that. But Rockne did that in pointing out how valuable college football was not only for the players who played but for the university. Where's the Notre Dame spirit today? I think it started—there was a lot of good spirit here before Rockne—but Rockne was the one who stimulated Notre Dame to where the spirit today is just as good as it was in my time. No question about that. Sure, the kids today have a lot more things to do than in my time when all we had was football and the auditorium for a movie. And that's about it. But now the kids have other diversified activities and extracurricular activities with the girls on campus and so on [Notre Dame began admitting female undergraduate students in the mid-70s]. But even now you go to one of our pep rallies and you'll see about the same things that happened in the Twenties or Thirties or Forties or Fifties or Sixties when Ara was here. It's still here today. But Rockne was so far ahead of people on promoting football through radio. And of course his speeches around the country and before clinics. He spoke at more clinics than all the coaches put together. And got the high school coaches and college coaches thinking not only of football as a revenue-producing sport, as a developer of men, he'd talk about athletics. You take our university here at Notre Dame now; we've got four out of every five boys or girls participating in some sport. We believe that there's a great value in **competition** in sports, not only the varsity team; we're talking about the club sports teams, the intramurals sports here on campus. And when he was here, we had a great intramural program. He started all this. We're one of the few schools in the country, outside of the service [academies], that has regular football in the inter-hall system. You say, "My gosh, a lot of injuries." No, there aren't too many injuries. They're well protected and fairly well coached. You take in 1930 when I was a freshman; there were seven, eight, nine hundred kids playing football. It's the same thing today. So, there is an interest here. But it also stimulates a great deal of pride in the alumni into having a winning team. We've been winning most of the time even since Rockne's death. We've had some bad years. This year (1979) some of the alumni think it's a bad year. Well, maybe next year it'll be a better one. We'll see. [Indeed, the Irish went from 7-4 in '79 to 9-2-1 in '80, Dan Devine's final season]. On the other hand, our alumni take pride in the fact that we have a winning football team. That's number one. . . . We're on radio and television more than any other schools because we believe in exposure, the public relations factor, to the university as a whole, not just the athletic department. It's been a tremendous thing; this was Rockne's thinking

STEELE: He was a master at that; just a master.

KRAUSE: He was a great actor.

STEELE: I'm glad you said that. You know he played here in the theater. He often had women's roles.

KRAUSE: Me too—in some show in the Monogram Absurdities.

STEELE: Did you? He invented that, didn't he?

KRAUSE: Yes. That's died down since then because the kids had so many things going on. We used to have to work like hell to get a show started, weeks and months to get a show ready.

STEELE: Well, how credible is the chorus line story? Do you think that there is an element of truth to that?

KRAUSE: Gee, I don't know. You might talk to Chet Grant about that. I've heard that. If there's any value to it, I think, it's the value that he might have got from the rhythm of the ballet dancers or chorus girls dancing. His shift was a beautiful thing to watch because it was all timing, just like a graceful chorus line actually.

STEELE: This is a hard one; I'm sorry to have to ask you this. We know that Rockne at the 1928 Army game asked the team to win one for the Gipper and we know that Jack Chevigny said, "That's one for the Gipper!" when he scored in the third quarter. Perhaps we can never know, no one else was there but Rockne and Gipp, but do you think Gipp actually said that?

KRAUSE: You know, Gipp would be the kind of person who would say that. He was so highly revered by his [fellow] players; he was much older, well, two or three years older, as you know. My high school coach played with him, Judge Norm Barry in Chicago, and the kids on the team, including [Barry], used to talk about how George Gipp was their real leader. He could gamble; he could do a lot of things. He told me a story once which was true, about a train ride to New York or someplace. In those days they had a barber on the train who would cut hair and shave people on the train but he was also a dice shark, a hustler. And he was in a dice game with some of the players and winning all the money. Norm Barry came to him, George Gipp was half asleep in his bunk there, and came up to him and said, "Hey, George, that barber in there is really taking the boys." He went in there and he could see that the barber had loaded dice. Of course, Gipp was so damned sharp, it was his turn to take the dice, and he put his own sort of dice in and won all the money and kicked the barber off the train (laughs) as they were slowing up at some station. That's the kind of thing that the kids had great respect for him. Or in a ball game, they always gave the ball to George when they were in trouble.

STEELE: So you think Gipp was the sort of person who could have said that?

KRAUSE: Yes. I think he had a great deal of love for his fellow players from the point of view that they were very close even then. We speak about the closeness and the family of our football teams. I would, yes, I think.

STEELE: Rockne, in his books and articles, often talks about masculine democracy at Notre Dame. What does this mean to you? In terms of your student years here in the thirties.

KRAUSE: Well, this was a man's school then. We felt we were a very select school from the point of view that it was a man's school. And we had a lot of fun here contrary to some of the youngsters today who don't think we enjoyed ourselves. We did. We didn't have any money, that's for sure. I got a buck a month to spend for my

Moose Krause and Frank Leahy when the Irish were undefeated over four seasons.

times. But we had a lot of fun, just having bull sessions around the campus. I had a lot of friends of mine who were nonathletes. A couple of kids from Spain and New Orleans who never played any football. But, as you know, on our campus, our athletes live in the regular halls and get to know the student body as well as they know us. We were treated more as students than as athletes in this sense. But I'd say in those days, yes, we had something that was much different than what it is today. Today, the kids on the football and basketball teams don't feel they're part of a family. We feel that this part of the campus, the athletic part of the campus, has more rules than say the campus itself. They've got to follow some kind of discipline, the rules of the coaches bring out to them that they have to follow. And, strange as it may seem, those kids today are looking for more discipline than ever before. Not only Notre Dame, but all schools have laxity in rules as far as the campus is concerned. But to be on a team, you have to make some sacrifices. These were the things that Rockne talked about too. You've got to make a sacrifice to become successful. You have to prove yourself every day in practice sessions. It's going to be tedious but you have to do it. And you have to devote some time and physical effort and mental effort to become a part of the team. So, we still have that here today. So, I say, even though we have the coeds on campus, in a sense we still have some masculinity in our athletic programs. I feel that way very strongly.

STEELE: To what extent did Rockne coach from the sidelines? Did the quarterback do most of it?

KRAUSE: Rockne used to do what Frank Leahy did afterwards and Ara Parseghian did afterwards. Rockne met with his quarterbacks practically every day. They knew his philosophy. For instance, at these noon meetings I brought up, he'd put the ball on the ten-yard line, we're here at third down and five yards to go, and you knew if you were in that position of the field, the quarterback knew the plays that would work on this kind of defense and so on. But the quarterbacks were so well schooled, very seldom did he have to send plays in, because the quarterbacks knew what Rockne had taught them regarding the type of play to be used in certain situations, the wind blowing like this, the wet field, how to stop the clock, and all that business. But the quarterbacks were called generals in our time. Frank Carideo, I remember him as a senior; cripes, he was a general out there.

STEELE: This is the man [a senior, an All-American] you knocked out as a freshman?

KRAUSE (laughing): Yeh, yeh, I thought I was going to be kicked off the squad. You read about that?

STEELE: It was in the last *Alumnus* magazine.

KRAUSE: But anyway, Rockne schooled his quarterbacks and met with them separately practically every day, whether it was the spring time—and our spring season started about January . . . .

STEELE: So they could do what they wanted but they knew his system.

KRAUSE: They knew his system. Occasionally, he'd send a play in, but not too often.

STEELE: Well, the rules then said that they had to wait one down before they could even say anything.

KRAUSE: You're right, in those days. They were so well schooled, they were just like a coach being on the field. You find that happening once in a while now in some of the games you see on TV. Some of the pro teams, not many college teams, will let the quarterback call it. Take a kid like Staubach or Griese; they know their systems. But Rockne schooled his quarterbacks so strongly, so consistently, that they knew exactly what play to run or what type of plays to run.

STEELE: He was apparently very scientific in his approach to the game. Would you agree with that?

KRAUSE: No question about it.

STEELE: Partially as a result of his own background in science? He trusted science.

KRAUSE: I would say yes. I would say that ... you go back to the game of muscle and brawn, and Rockne's intelligence led him to believe a scientific mind would be better. He used the talents of his players. They didn't have to be big as long as they were quick and smart, very smart. His players were no different than now. They talk about so many defenses that players have to watch, the linemen as well as the backs, defenses they have to watch, the way they line up, how they shift along the line. Rockne had the linemen as well as the backs schooled to the point where they knew if a man moved here that he'd be your assignment instead of mine. It was just an automatic thing. In fact, in my time, when Rockne coached, we never had a huddle, very seldom used a huddle.

STEELE: Now that surprised me. I didn't know that until [recently]. As soon as the play was over you just picked yourself up and went back to the line.

KRAUSE: To the line. And that not only saved a lot of time, you ran more plays. The point was that the linemen had to be intelligent, too, because the quarterback would call a certain set of signals—he would call 45-19-62—and that means fifty-one to the right. [The second and third digits designate the number of the play, fifty-one, and another number designates whether it is to go right or left.] All the other teams used huddles even in those days, so he was way advanced.

STEELE: I've read about his signal-calling techniques. They're tough; I can readily agree with it. Just reading through it once, I didn't catch on. I had to go back and read it again.

KRAUSE: You finally got it (laughs).

STEELE: Yeh, I got it. Tough.

KRAUSE: Well, if you can get it, anyone can get it. (Chuckles.)

STEELE: (laughing): Well, probably. Now, don't you think that Rockne eventually won what was called the overemphasis battle? You know, the Carnegie report, certain faculty members on campus and nationally. It seems to me he won that. Would you agree?

KRAUSE: Oh, no question about that. In fact, it's been going on. He'd been unfairly criticized after he left, more than when he lived here and coached here, that we were a football factory. The only reason we were named a football factory was because everyone is convinced that to have a winning team you've got to be cheating, that you've got to have kids who just can play football. But that's not true. The perfect answer to that is when you can look at the record of our Notre Dame athletes graduating, when 99.5 percent of them graduate in four years. There's no question in anyone's mind that Notre Dame is [a leader in this regard]. But it's taken a long time. With the great advent of Father Hesburgh, who's done a tremendous job of elevating our academic standing around the world. It's been a wonderful thing to know now that the NCAA, as an example, gave Notre Dame as the perfect example of what we should do with our athletic programs. Just recently they had Jack Fusack, president of the NCAA, retired now, now carrying on a survey of how many boys graduate from schools around the NCAA. It's a sad figure, a sad figure. So he was here to find out how we do it. Every place I've gone, [for instance] the president of Texas asked me years ago, "How can you do that? " So many of them are red-shirting—holding them back a year. We don't do that here unless a boy gets hurt and requests that. It isn't a coach saying, "You've got to stay." The boy can graduate with his class. And some of the kids who get hurt, because of the additional year, we allow that. But the proof of the pudding is that Notre Dame is now being used as an example by the NCAA to point out to these other schools who are beating the rules in a sense and not giving the boys a college education, that there's a way of doing this, and there is.

STEELE: So, do you think that there's a relationship between Rockne and academic excellence?

KRAUSE: There is, because Rockne believed that. The first story I told you, the first question he asked me. He

Pat O'Brien with Moose Krause.

didn't know it was my dad there! "Moose, how're you doing in your studying?" And I was only a freshman. And, doggone it, I know he was concerned about all his players. The *Sports Illustrated* survey taken many years ago about what's happened to Notre Dame players. You'd be amazed, in Rockne's day, we had as many graduates then as now. But people are finding out now that Notre Dame wins and still has boys who are qualified to get an education and to receive one. We don't have any soft courses here at Notre Dame. Never had.

STEELE: I didn't find any. I was scared my freshman year.

KRAUSE: Everybody is.

STEELE: Now, my last question; apparently the Kansas newspapers at the time of his death and Father Cavanaugh's epilogue to the *Autobiography* stated that Rockne, when they found the body, was clutching his rosary. Is that true?

KRAUSE: That's what I've heard.

INTERVIEW WITH CHET GRANT

This interview was arranged for the author by Mr. Herb Juliano, then curator of the Sports and Games Research Collection at Notre Dame. Chet Grant had been instrumental in founding this collection in the mid-sixties. He has been a fixture around Notre Dame football since before Gipp's playing days. In correspondence with me before my trip to South Bend in 1979, Grant had graciously agreed to have an interview but advised me to read his book on football at Notre Dame before the advent of Rockne. This, he asserted, would give me the necessary background to carry out the interview. This task dutifully performed, I waited eagerly for his opportunity to meet the one man who has seen more Notre Dame football than anyone alive.

While working with materials housed in the collection on December 18, 1979, Herb Juliano advised me that Mr. Grant would drop by that day. We met that afternoon in Mr. Juliano's office in the Memorial Library's Special Collections section. The first impression that one has of Chet Grant is his diminutive size—perhaps 5 feet, 6 inches or so—but this he carries with a certain cockiness. His face shows his eighty-odd years with grace and firmness. His jaw is held with a measure of determination and grit. When the interview began, it was notable that he was thinking over each response carefully, deliberately. His answers were almost whispered. At one point he asked that the tape recorder be turned off while he mulled over a question. Having organized his thoughts, we launched back into the interview. Grant seems to be very aware of the important place he holds in Notre Dame tradition and thus chooses his words with care so as to avoid imprecision. It is unfortunate that after the conclusion of the interview proper, we carried on informally without the tape recorder being on. Eventually, as we warmed to the technical subject of the shift, we moved from the office into an area housing expensive special collections. Amid the towering glass-enclosed shelves, I was put through the paces that Grant ordered as we assumed various

Chet Grant

positions in order to execute the shift. He carefully showed how the backs would move from the basic T-formation into the dreaded Notre Dame box. It was an amusing, interesting, and very informative session—a bridge across generations, a "practice" reminiscent of the mythical sessions held by Rockne as he utilized family members, furniture, anything at hand, to work out an idea in his living room. The old Notre Dame shift, long dead as a football tactic, came alive for those moments for me; I would only see old films of it later during the research process. In sum, I view this demonstration with respectful awe, a privileged moment when the ideas of Knute Rockne were transmitted through one of his players, a former teammate of George Gipp.

STEELE: One of the things that I noticed in your book was that you said had Rockne lived long enough, he would have righted some fabrications that had come out. What, for instance, were some of those fabrications?

GRANT: Yes. That the Notre Dame football tradition started with Rockne. That's the main one. I think I indicated that very clearly in the book. He made the most of what he found here. That was his function. He probably exceeded the capacity of anybody else who ever came along. If those successors, any of them, no matter how

Chet Grant

talented, had come along, none of them would have been quite the right man for that particular point in time. That's my conclusion from a long-term acquaintance with the background of Notre Dame football.

STEELE: In your dealings with Rockne, as a human being, what would you say was his most important personal characteristic?

GRANT: I would say—I've said it in the book—his most important trait, if trait's the right word for it, he was the very essence of dedication. He was a humble man. Humility, I've indicated in the book, in humility, there is strength. And there isn't really true strength without humility. When you go to the other extreme, it's pride. As far as Roman Catholics are concerned, I imagine other Christians, maybe non-Christians, I don't know, pride is defined definitely as a sin. It's a traitor to anybody. There's no such thing as good pride or not-so-bad pride. It either is or isn't. I mean essentially, supernaturally. And, after all, if there is an afterlife, we have to be concerned with what is supernaturally thought of. That's my association with Rock. He could have all kinds of human failings. Hasty temper, on occasions. But humility saved him. An example would be having some difficulty with a particular player, and he would either throw the player off the squad or the player would quit. Now if the player didn't show up on a Monday after a game, and again, Rock would then send somebody, an emissary, to invite him to come over. And you know those guys saved face from that. Well, there it was—a Christian attitude. I don't think that term was used in his own mind at all. It's just the way he was. If he were afflicted with false pride he wouldn't do that. He might have hurt both of them by holding a grudge.

STEELE: One of the little myths about Rockne is in the report that, when they found his body at the crash site, he was clutching a rosary.

GRANT: That's very probable. In a sense, I was in the same spiritual boat as him except that he was not baptized originally as a Catholic. I was, but was never raised as a Catholic. I think you saw that in the book. I would say if I were going somewhere under similar circumstances today I'm pretty sure I'd have my rosary handy. I often carry it. I have been carrying it for decades. I feel lost without it.

STEELE: So he probably did the same thing then.

GRANT: Yes, I would think so.

STEELE: What do you think he meant to the average undergraduate, say from 1920 to 1930? If you could

try to capture it. Was he a role model for these people?

GRANT: I don't know. I can't put myself in the position of an undergraduate hardly at any time. Because I was twenty-three years old when I came to Notre Dame and I was out from the spring of 1918 to the fall of 1920. So, when I came back I was twenty-eight and played my last game when I was twenty-nine. So I can't identify too much with the conventional academic outlook in college.

STEELE: What was Rockne's relationship with people in South Bend, away from the campus?

GRANT: He would go downtown habitually, and he would seek out the opinions of these followers, the downtown quarterbacks, the Monday morning coaches, the downtown coaches, and the like. And he would argue with them and sometimes they would come up with something he'd agree with, but he'd never let them know it. But he wouldn't scrap it. He'd go out and try it out and see if it had something. A proud man wouldn't have done that. He'd just have scorned it and just said, "Why these dummies—they couldn't think of anything to be of value to us. We're professionals." But he wasn't that way. And, of course, that was his general attitude toward all people. I think he greatly respected the human factors.

STEELE: I think I understand what happened with the backs in the shift. What happened with the linemen?

GRANT: As a matter of fact, they ruled against the ends participating in the shift. It was against the rules for them to shift in your time [the sixties]. Before that too.

STEELE: When the linemen were allowed to shift. [Note: I'm in the process of losing a misperception here].

GRANT: Not the linemen; just the ends.

STEELE: Just the ends? It wasn't the interior linemen?

GRANT: No. Although the only place where they might be an exception would be the pulling guard. He anticipated just a trifle to pull out of there. By the rule he should not move until the ball's snapped. Now, the end could shift with the backs. And he either maintained the position to which he shifted or he only faked it and on the second count he'd come back to the original position, depending on whether he'd block in or block out. And he'd mix them up, you see. There was a lot of flexibility; it was very

Chet Grant, after he helped found the Sports and
Games Research Collection.

Jesse Harper receiving an award from Father Edmund P. Joyce.

valuable. But they got rid of that in Rockne's time. They did other things. They put that second stop on the shift. But he continued to use it effectively, although they tell me he'd installed some spin stuff. Some historians and even some players are quoted as it having been used effectively as early as the mid-twenties. I was coaching high school and we were still doing those things. Not long after that, before Rock died, they put the quietus on the shifting ends as well as the added stop.

STEELE: In Stuhldreher's book, he claims that Rockne got some of the inspiration for the shift from a chorus line. I just want to know your opinion.

GRANT (growling): Don't make me ... don't arouse me. Ridiculous. He's probably commenting on it. The shift was already installed and working.

STEELE: Harper had it too, didn't he?

GRANT: Oh yes. Well, I have a letter from Harper some place in which he thinks they began to try it out in 1913, during Rock's senior year. In 1914 they started the season without it for the simple reason, it seems logical to me, the quarterback indicated for the 1914 season hadn't returned to school as yet when they went to play Yale. As a result, Coffall, the halfback, undertook to call the signals. And that didn't beat us. What I'm getting at is that they didn't use it until this other man, Dutch Bergman, came back and took over. And I'm sure they used it. In an exchange of correspondence with Dutch Bergman he said that he used the shift against Syracuse. They had to be working on it before that. Now I know this about it, in 1915, I entered Notre Dame...but didn't go out for freshman ball. In the spring of 1915, that was my first football practice. And the shift then was as it was from there on until the rules changed. Now, however, I understand that the shifting ends had been installed prior to my first spring practice. In 1915 they were using shifting ends, and maybe earlier, maybe even in 1914. And there's a difference of recollection as to who was responsible. Rockne was given credit, and then Mal Elward, who was an end in 1913 and 1914, and who was small, only 140, a very doughty young man, good competitor. He is identified by some, and whether that includes himself or not I don't know. But certainly it was functioning then. And, out of my experience, I assumed that was part of it.

STEELE: We know what Rock said to the players in the 1928 Army game. And we know that the halfback said, "That's one for the Gipper!"

GRANT: That was Chevigny.

STEELE: Yes, now do you think that Gipp made the request? You knew Gipp and you knew Rock.

GRANT: I think it's credible, highly credible. Not only that, but I have a friend, Ed Healy, a Dartmouth man, who donated his services to Rock on the field. He was there in the dressing room and so testified a couple of times in my presence when this sequence occurred. He said that's the way it was. And, anyhow, no matter whether he had or not, I would have to answer I don't see why not. At the time I rejected it. I never heard Gipp referred to as Gipper before. I thought it was an affectation of some kind. In retrospect, considering all that could be involved, I see no reason why it shouldn't be accepted or to try to explain it. What's the difference?

STEELE: That's one of the things that I'm working with. So many things have become facts, are taken to be facts, by people in later generations.

GRANT: Well, it's the essence of it that counts. So, that's not contrary to the credible.

STEELE: Since I came here, I've learned that there was a brother in the room [with Gipp and Rockne]. I don't have his name, but somebody remembers him.

GRANT: Well, I don't know about it. I'd have to question it myself. Sometimes fables become facts in time. Sometimes witnesses have heard the fable so often that they've translated it. [This is a crucial observation in the study of the life of Knute Rockne.]

STEELE: Yes. Now, do you think that Rock won the battle in the overemphasis issue?

GRANT: How do you mean?

STEELE: Through the mid-Twenties and up to the Carnegie Report number 23, which said that football was overemphasized, over commercialized, and overprofessionalized.

GRANT: In what fashion do you expect him to combat that?

Mrs. Rockne with
Hunk Anderson.

STEELE: Well, he argued in various speeches and various articles that battle. That is, football as we know it and its impact on our society and in our colleges, seems to be about the same as in the Twenties. Do you agree?

GRANT: Oh well, except for the commitment all along the line has changed so greatly in the colleges as self-defense against the rules. There are two groups of men; you have to double the size of the squad—I mean of the men that they expect to produce. In Elmer Layden's time [mid-Thirties], his requests for money ... no. Overemphasis has not been spiked. The institution, no matter what the actual case was, the institution was overemphasis-oriented when Rockne died. And during Hunk Anderson's time, Hunk claims that they began to de-emphasize by taking away some of his scholarships. And then Elmer Layden inherited not only that factual phase of fear of overemphasis or impression of overemphasis. But he countered it anyhow in other ways, academically. In his time they raised the academic eligibility age for a job scholarship, an athletic scholarship, which was then contingent upon a job, from 75 [percent] to 77 [percent—grade averages] for job holders among the athletes. And Elmer did a number of other things.

INTERVIEW WITH PAUL CASTNER

Paul Castner

This interview was held on December 28, 1979. Castner had dropped by the Special Collections area earlier when I was not expecting him; my tape recorder was not there. We chatted as I took notes and then asked Castner to return for a follow-up. He graciously accepted the invitation and then left me with a copy of his book, *We Remember Rockne.*

The actual interview recorded here took place in the spacious reading room of the Special Collections. Like many of the tomes that filled the shelves, Dante and the like, Castner is a legend that takes on more significance with the passage of time. As mentioned earlier, he was one of four men who were the "hinges" or connecting points between the Gipp era and the Four Horsemen era. In 1979, he was the only survivor of that group and of that group was the only one to maintain a close relationship with Rockne. At Notre Dame he played three sports— football, baseball, hockey—and still possesses the Notre

Dame record for yards averaged in a season for kick-off returns, an amazing 35.5 yards per return. He did this without benefit of having played the game before entering college. His first encounter with the game was in Europe, where he won a kicking award in the AEF sports program. Upon his return to the United States, a friend told him that he could probably go on to college at Notre Dame, where there was a coach who could use Castner's raw talents and make him into a good player. So, like Rockne and Gipp, he went to South Bend without much money or extensive experience with the game of football. With much practice, he became the starting fullback beside Gipp for the 1920 season. It was his broken hip in the 1922 Butler game that provided Rockne the opportunity to switch around some young players, all sophomores that season, who became the Four Horsemen when Grantland Rice christened them in 1924.

After completing his education, Castner played professional baseball as a pitcher with the Chicago White Sox. His greatest moment in this game was when he had faced Ty Cobb, who walked, stole second, stole third, and then threatened to steal home. Castner, the rookie, and Cobb, the wizened veteran, played a game of exposed nerves as Castner tried to pitch to the Sox batter with Cobb faking steals from third. At the right moment, Cobb sped home and Castner's throw was too late. Castner eventually came to be known as Mr. Hockey for the sport that genuinely claimed his heart in college. He was the most instrumental person in the development of the Irish hockey program. Finally, it was Castner who recommended to Studebaker officials that they had in South Bend the hottest item for public speaking in the country—Rockne. For three years, Castner and Rockne traveled the circuit in the off season going from dealers' meeting to conventions to car shows with Rockne providing the entertainment and inspiration to flattered, adulatory Studebaker dealers and salesmen. Castner was one of the last people in South Bend to see Rockne alive when they parted at the Studebaker offices just prior to Rockne's trip West. Since then, Castner has spoken to countless groups about his former coach. In the 1960s, he realized that many of the greats from the Rockne era were passing on. He undertook a project of traveling across the country in his RV to meet and interview the fading luminaries. The results of this arduous work may be found in *We Remember Rockne*, which provides some of the most pertinent personal recollections of Rockne on record.

Like Chet Grant, Castner was in his eighties when I came to know him. One's first impression is of his massive chest, fine, firm head, and, perhaps most interesting, his very large but expressive hands. He spoke forcefully, almost poetically, of his recollections. He is a man of firm opinions and very conscious of being one of the last guardians of the Rockne legacy. He was not a revisionist with regard to the memory of Rockne. Indeed, it has been his self-appointed duty to see that the Rockne he knew and loved comes to later generations in the religious, chivalric mode that was used in the Twenties. This does not make his views obsolete because it is likely that his articulation of the Rockne legend was as truthful as any offered by a writer who never met the great coach. Finally, it must be reiterated that the views of Grant and Castner did not always agree; there was a degree of professional jealousy between the two men—which might be expected given their different relationships to the coach. They tended to agree on the essentials. The difference was the degree to which they went in attributing sheer inventiveness to Rockne. Grant held firmly that Rockne built upon what already existed at Notre Dame.

Castner tended to avoid technical matters related to football in order to concentrate his views on somewhat more abstract matters, such as Rockne's religious impact. Both men were probably right in certain ways; the territory is large enough, to be sure, for the views of both to flourish.

STEELE: Could you state your opinions on Rockne's importance because of his religious contribution?

CASTNER: Yes. I believe, great as Rockne's contributions are to the game of football—and he's still voted as the greatest in the history of the game, and he's got a fabulous record, and of course his knowledge of football is great—but I believe that his greatest contribution to America was in the spiritual field. I say that advisedly. When he came to Notre Dame, they had thirty-five hours of philosophy in the old bachelor's degree where you had Latin, Greek, and they studied where we came from and where we're going. And God was in education. That was the bachelor's degree. That stuck with Rockne. When I arrived here [1919] there were nineteen hours of philosophy. It wasn't quite the same thing. But, at any rate, the schools like Harvard, Yale, Princeton, Chicago, Northwestern, and all these schools had a church background originally. And then they came in with the Ph.D. and they eliminated God. Now Rockne came into the picture and he made this statement: "I do not want to belittle the cultural advantages of a college education, but nowhere in the classroom do the boys get the give-and-take that they get on the athletic field, nor do they learn the practical lessons for life as well as they do on the playing field." Now heretofore the physical was never related with education. But now here Rockne takes this and relates it to education. He spells it out when he talks about the lesson: he says that sacrifice, team play, getting along with your fellow man, the ability to win graciously, the ability to lose gracefully—a little tougher—and the will to win, standing in to the last whistle and all these things. He gave all these a spiritual quality and made them part of the educational system. When I say that this was the first time in the history of the world that this took place, you study the history of the physical, go back to Rome and Greece, and you'll find that it was often brutal. I mean the gladiators.

The bust of Knute Rockne that resides in the building named after the legendary coach.

It never related to education. And as it came through the years it was never related to education. The Olympic Games were feats of endurance more than anything else. And in England they said the Battle of Waterloo was won on the playing fields of Eton. But you weren't on the playing fields of Eton unless you had a lot of money. You had a class society formed on a horizontal basis. You couldn't come up through those layers.

[For instance,] here's a Greek, a captain in the Air Force, World War II, and they were interviewing him and got down to the $64,000 question: "Do you like America?" He said, "I love it." Why?" He said, "Because if I was in Greece I couldn't be in the Air Force."

Now that's hard to believe. And I've talked to a lot of youngsters, and I've told them they ought to get down on their knees and thank the Lord they're in America. You could come from here (points downward) and go to the top.

Now Rockne came in and he was a catalyst that took the physical and made it part of the educational system. And that's what I mean when I speak of his greatest contribution to America. You see, the old bachelor's degree was character formation and the belief in God. He made athletes, he made the physical part of culture formation. And of course in my own personal experience and having had such a very close relationship with Rockne, and in the automobile business when I got Studebaker to hire him, we went from the Bronx to the Bowery and all over the United States and I lived in the same hotel rooms with this man. And I never, ever saw him do one untoward thing. He was a beautiful man, just a beautiful man.

STEELE: So you think that in addition to teaching, what you've just spoken of, it was part and parcel of his personality, his character.

CASTNER: That's right. You'll find in my book where they have the story of his talk to the Studebaker dealers. He talks about when he starts the boys out and he talks to them about ambition and he says most of what he's read about ambition is a lot of bunk. "There isn't plenty of room at the top. There's room at the top for the few only that roll up their sleeves." And then he said, "Later on, I talk to them about perseverance." He said, "Because no ambition is worthwhile unless you have perseverance." And his illus-

Knute Rockne and A.R. Erskine, president of Studebaker.

tration of perseverance: "I was going to the Player's Club in New York with Lawrence Perry, the author. It was started by Edwin Booth, the playwright. And under his leadership it became a great club. As we were going through the club we came to a room, the room in which Booth would want to read and study. One day sitting there he died. And they left the room as it was, and the book open to where he was reading at the time of his death. And I went over and glanced out of curiosity to find out what he was reading. It was Pope's "Essay on Man." And then, the very gracious Rockne aside said, "You all remember it." He said, "Pope's 'Essay on Man' came from the Greek scholars, the greatest scholars of them all, Aristotle and the rest of them. Because they said the greatest study of man was mankind. And Pope's 'Essay on Man' relates back to those scholars." Well, here's just a football coach in there quoting out of Pope's "Essay on Man." And he used that. He said, "Hope springs eternal in the human breast" is the first line. And the last line, "If hope eludes you all is lost."

Now I liken this to the miners of old who would sift the sands of the streams for tiny flecks of gold. Rockne sifted the sands of time for flecks of wisdom, which he applied to his own life and joyously passed on to those who came under his influence.

STEELE: Father Cavanaugh, in his remarks in the *Autobiography*, said that Rockne had all of his life suffered from intellectual starvation. He was constantly reading.

CASTNER: His mind was constantly hungry for knowledge. That story I just told is an indication of the thinking, his knowledge, and his study of history. He always had books with him. When we traveled around for Studebaker he had two or three books with him all the time. He had a little variety.

STEELE: You've said that he had "the soul of a poet." Could you elaborate on that?

CASTNER: Well, I was talking about his statement with reference to the shift. ... Let's get that quote right. (Looks for his book.) The lilt and nuance of the Hungarian gypsy . . . .

STEELE: Yes, I remember that now.

CASTNER: The lilt and nuance of the Hungarian gypsy and then the Chester Hale Girls. Here it is. (Points it out in the book.)

STEELE: Yes, that's it. It's in his shift article. Now, could you tell me about your position with Studebaker?

CASTNER: When I got out of [Notre Dame] I finished the season with the Chicago White Sox. And then I came down here in 1923 and I went to work for Studebaker. They started a new commercial division. I was a junior executive; I was the assistant sales manager of the new commercial division. Rockne was making some talks. He made a talk up in Detroit, I remember that. To the Graham brothers. They had gone to Notre Dame. Knowing Rockne was such a great talker I went in to see Paul Hoffmann, who was the vice-president in charge of sales, and

I said, "You're letting the best speaker in the country get away." We talked about how to use him. I said, "Well, the automobile show, the dealer's meeting, the salesman's meeting. He's got great magnetism because he's a great talker." Acting on that, he hired Rockne and paid him five thousand dollars just to go around and start the New York Automobile Show. Then I traveled with him and I talked on the commercial cars. We had the passenger car sales manager, the engineer, me, and then Rockne. And so in 1929 he had phlebitis and he didn't go out. In 1930 Hoffmann called me into his office and said he wanted to get all of Rockne's time except for what he wanted for himself and Notre Dame. In other words, his spare time. Just wanted to get competitive business out of him. I said, "What'll you pay him?" Well, Rockne at that time was doing some shorts for movies; Pathe news had him on explaining football. He says, "Well, if he hasn't got movie stars' ideas of salary, I think we can go on." I said, "How much?" He said, "Ten thousand dollars." You've heard of the "message of Garcia"? Well, you should have seen Castner heading for the Rockne home. (Laughs.) He's getting ten thousand dollars from Notre Dame and this [offer] is just for his spare time!

The Rockne Six, by Studebaker.

STEELE: You should have collected a finder's fee or something.

CASTNER: Oh, I took the president of Studebaker out to Mrs. Rockne's home after his death, and he graciously asked her permission to bring out the Rockne car, which was a light six named for Rockne. That was produced for two years, and she got about thirty-five thousand dollars in royalties on that. So I was responsible for bringing about fifty thousand dollars into the Rockne home.

STEELE: I just saw an article on that car. A man down in Dallas has one. About thirty thousand of them were made in 1932 and 1933. I've read recently that Studebaker made a short advertisement, a movie advertisement, of Rockne, and a recording of him was made talking to salesmen. Do you know of any Studebaker archives where these things might be located?

CASTNER: No. I have copies of some of the letters he wrote. They're at home. I can get them. I have storage space up there with files of the stuff. And I have in there the Studebaker files and some of the letters that he wrote. They had an outfit that specialized in training. This guy's name was Osborne, the head of it. He would give Rockne the lesson, and Rockne would add the flavor of Rockne.

STEELE: Do you think that if Rockne had lived that the history of the Studebaker Corporation might have been different?

CASTNER: No. He had nothing to do with it.

STEELE: Do you think that Studebaker might still have gone downward gradually?

CASTNER: Yes, because he didn't have anything to say about the management. He was just hired to be a specialist in inspiring them. Well, of course, it could help, but I don't think that would have made a difference. [This is an interesting point from the perspective of a person from within a major corporation. It contrasts quite starkly with the views put forth by McCready Huston, who saw in Rockne and his methods a veritable savior for the depressed economy of 1931 America.]

STEELE: It seems to me that there are two schools of thought about Rockne—mainly represented by you and Mr. Grant. I'm wondering if you have any observations on how these two schools of thought came into being? One rather downplays Rockne's role.

CASTNER: The only place they downplay it was the fact that they said he didn't originate anything, that everything was there and all he did was just improve it. Now, unfortunately, if you weren't on your toes you'd think sometimes you were doing Rockne's thinking for him. Because he'd ask questions and probe and be very gracious in always giving credit to people. [This does not match Grant's note that Rockne borrowed some football ideas from the good citizens of South Bend without telling them.] Here's Alonzo Stagg on the Rules Committee. Under Stagg, they started after Rockne in 1922, 1925, 1927, and 1929 when they passed rulings. Rock was still gracious to the guy. There wasn't a mean bone in the guy's body, but he was giving credit to other people. And in this framework, he'd say he got the shift from Stagg. Well, I have quotes from Jess Harper in the *Autobiography*. At any rate, Harper, who should know, spoke of who first used the shift. And he said that Stagg made some use of it, but he said that Notre Dame was the first one that, from the standard T-formation, developed a full offensive on the backfield shift. Now, he says specifically that Stagg made some use of it. And Stagg was using tackles back and guards back. And when Harper, even talking about the shift then, he talked about the Doc Williams shift up in Minnesota. Now in the Doc Williams shift, the whole line came back about two yards back of the line of scrimmage. Of course, it was the same thing when Stagg used it with tackles back and guards back. They would take two steps forward and just stop for a second and keep on going. Now this is a momentum shift. Rockne had the first nonmomentum shift. And Stagg never used anything of that kind. Harper turned most of the running of the team, substitutions, and pep talks, and everything else—he had Rockne do it. Harper's great credit is the fact that he recognized in Rockne what a great guy he was. I don't want to get into this downgrading Harper at all because he deserved great credit for turning things over to Rockne. And the shift, the Notre Dame shift, was developed by Rockne, period. He had the flexing ends and everything else Now he developed this. This is what these guys won't give Rockne credit for. I can't understand it at all.

STEELE: I was wondering why that might be happening.

CASTNER: Because he was so gracious. He gave everybody else the credit. He was always so generous. And it's unfortunate. It's just a few people who downgrade him on this. I had Jimmy Phelan and Charlie Bachman over at the Morris Inn [the campus guest lodging], and these two guys wouldn't give him credit for anything. I finally said, "You've got to give him credit for the flexing ends." And they finally did, you see.

STEELE: I understand that you're concerned with the issue of violence in sports. Isn't it the view that the shift removed much of the prior levels of violence from football?

CASTNER: Well, Rockne … I base my thinking … Rockne was a wise man, and when he made an observation it was usually very solid. He said that the shift is a great equalizer between the big and little teams. It enabled the smaller man to play on equal terms with the bigger man.

A pensive Rockne.

STEELE: In your personal relationship with him, what do you think was his greatest strength in human relationships, whether with a football player or a person in the street?

CASTNER: Well, it was his genuine interest in all of them. It didn't have to be a George Gipp; it could be a little third stringer. He was an all-out man in being real helpful. Of course, he set the pace. The first talk I heard him make at Notre Dame here when I went out for spring practice, and you're waiting for this guy to talk about blocking and tackling and football, and he opens up in a very low-key manner. "You're out for football which is fine, but most of you are here at considerable personal sacrifice on the part of your parents. The first thing you have to do is get your education. And after you get that then football is all right." That set the pace. He didn't make pious statements and not follow through. He followed through. He had his arm around us all the way through school helping us. And then right after we got out of school he was helping us.

STEELE: Have you any final thoughts on all of this?

CASTNER: We've covered the waterfront pretty well. (Pause.) He was just a beautiful man. Of course, here I am at eighty-two years of age, and I love him like a father.

STEELE: Almost every man I've talked to has used that word, father.

CASTNER: Chick Meehan [the former NYU coach] had one of the nicest little compliments for Rockne. Chick was an All-American at Syracuse, and then he was president of the Coach's Association. He coached Manhattan and NYU. He and Jimmy Crowley used to have great games there between Fordham and NYU. Well, anyway, Chick was a good friend of Rockne. But he'd shake hands and he'd say, "There's something about you Rockne men." That's a real compliment. Well, he left his stamp on me, for heaven's sake. What I am, my whole life, has been sparked by my love and affection for this guy.

STEELE: I told you that the word "father" comes up so much. But the other word, and you've used both of them now, is the word "something." The writers used it, the radio broadcasters used it, Moose Krause used it: "There was something about the man." I think it's an intangible, almost undefinable thing.

CASTNER: That's right. Chick Meehan perceived it.

ROCKNE AND THE NOTRE DAME RECORD BOOK

Mrs. Rockne, center, receiving an award in her husband's honor.

Knute Rockne coached the Fighting Irish from 1918 to 1930, a mere thirteen seasons, nearly three-quarters of a century ago. Yet his imprint is found throughout the Irish record book.

For instance, as of January, 1998, Notre Dame has played 1,023 football games. There have been 26 head coaches at Notre Dame. Rockne was the head coach for 122 games, winning 105 of them, losing 12, tying 5. Of ND's 753 career wins, Rockne has almost 14%. Of ND's 228 losses, he claims only 5%.

Examined further, we see that Rockne also coached three other Irish head coaches (Hunk Anderson, Elmer Layden, and Frank Leahy), and they coached several others—Hugh Devore, Terry Brennan, and Joe Kuharich. It may be said that Rockne's *direct* influence (his games plus the men he coached) influenced an incredible amount of Notre Dame's football history. Nearly 42% of all games played by Notre Dame have been under his direct or indirect influence. With his wins, those of the men he coached, and the

wins of their players, 41.5% of all Irish wins may be traced through Rockne. He and these men have coached 31.8% of ND's 108 seasons. Rockne himself has nearly 42% of all of ND's undefeated, untied seasons. Rockne plus Leahy have one half of all of Notre Dame's 12 undefeated/untied seasons. Of 28 Irish seasons with only 1 loss, Rockne coached six of them.

The four largest crowds for away games played by the Irish were played under Rockne—all four at Soldier Field—with USC in 1927 and 1929, Navy in 1928, and Army in 1930.

Notre Dame has had 77 consensus All-Americans. Rockne coached one as an assistant coach, 9 more as head coach, two others who earned these honors after his death, another 15 by those coaches who played for him, and another three by men they coached. Of the 77 consensus All-Americans, Rockne thus had an impact on 30 of those great players.

Frank Leahy, former head coach at Notre Dame.

Several of his players went on to distinguished careers as coaches in the collegiate and professional ranks. They include: Eddie Anderson, Curly Lambeau, Frank Thomas, Buck Shaw, Adam Walsh, Elmer Layden, Hunk Anderson, Jim Crowley, Slip Madigan, Harry Mehre, Jack Chevigny, and Frank Leahy.

Football has changed greatly over the years, but Rockne's players are still prominently represented in the Irish record book, including several who were not full-time starters:

George Gipp: 5th all-time leading rusher (whose rushing records lasted for more than half a century); 2nd in career rushing yards per game; 1st for rushing yards per attempt for a season; 1st in kickoff returns for a game; 1st in total kick returns in a game; 5th in career kickoff yards per attempt; 2nd in all-purpose yards rushing in a game.

Paul Castner: 1st in kickoff returns in a game; 5th in career kickoff return yards; 1st in kickoff return yards per attempt in a season and for a career; tied with 5 others as 1st for kickoff returns for TDs; 2nd for kick return yards in a game; 2nd in punting average for a game.

Red Maher: 2nd for points scored in a game (5 TDs); 3rd for kickoff return yardage in a game; 1st for kick return yardage in a game; 1st for all-purpose yards rushing in a game.

Jack Elder: longest interception return for a TD—100 yards, 1929.

Frank Carideo: 2nd for season interception yardage; 2nd for career punt returns; 2nd for punt return yards per attempt; 2nd in career total kick returns; 2nd in total kick return yardage in a game; 5th in career kick return yardage.

Chet Grant: 1st for punt return yards per attempt in a game.

Vince McNally: tied for 1st with 2 kickoff returns for TDs in a game.

Gene Edwards: 2nd for punt returns in a season.

Harry Stuhldreher: tied for 3rd for consecutive pass completions in a game (9); 3rd for career punt returns; 3rd for total kick returns in a career.

Rockne's defenses were absolutely stultifying and will remain in the record books probably for as long as the records are maintained. Consider the following staggering statistics:

Fewest rushing yards allowed per game in a season—45 yards, 1921.

Fewest rushing yards allowed per attempt in a season—1.4 yards, 1921.

Lowest pass completion percentage in a season—.215 (14 of 65), 1924.

Fewest TD passes allowed per game—0 (!!), 1921, 1922, 1924.

Fewest total yards of offense allowed in a season—651 (!!), 1924.

Fewest total offense yards per attempt for a season—1.8 yards (468 attempts for 843 yards), 1921.

Fewest first downs allowed in a season—42, 1924.

Fewest first downs allowed by passing in a season—8, 1924.

So, Rockne's teams could beat you with rushing, passing, special teams, or defense. This doesn't leave much for an opposing coach to hope for. These stats clearly reveal the wisdom behind Rockne's strategy of looking for scoring opportunities at any time. In a way, he reduced football to the basic maxim—my team will score and yours won't.

We may never live to see another coach dominate the game in the way Rockne did.